ECE/TRADE/185

United Nations
Economic Commission for Europe
Geneva

International Labour Organisation
Geneva

MANAGEMENT DEVELOPMENT IN EAST-WEST JOINT VENTURES:

A guide for managers in the economies in transition

UNITED NATIONS
New York, 1993

HD
38.25
.E852
M3
1993

United Nations
Economic Commission for Europe
Geneva

International Labour Organisation
Geneva

MANAGEMENT DEVELOPMENT IN EAST-WEST JOINT VENTURES

A guide for managers in the economies in transition

ECE/TRADE/185

UNITED NATIONS PUBLICATION
Sales No. E.93.II.E.18
ISBN 92-1-116567-9

UNITED NATIONS
New York, 1993

NOV 2 5 1993

MANAGEMENT DEVELOPMENT IN EAST-WEST JOINT VENTURES: A GUIDE FOR MANAGERS IN THE ECONOMIES IN TRANSITION

TABLE OF CONTENTS

PREFACE

Improving the quality of management is a <u>sine qua non</u> for the success of economic reform in central and eastern Europe and is accordingly one of the principal policy objectives of governments of the region. However, these governments have neither the resources nor the sufficient know-how to accomplish this objective easily or quickly. Western governments have also identified as a priority in their technical assistance to the region the need to train eastern European managers in market-oriented business techniques, but recognize that their own resources will be inadequate given the scale of this task. Hence, much emphasis is being placed on the contribution which private-sector western companies can make to management development in the countries of central and eastern Europe.

The Committee on the Development of Trade of the United Nations Economic Commission for Europe (UN/ECE) actively engages in monitoring and analyzing the development of East-West joint ventures and foreign direct investment projects. Its activities in this field include the periodic organization of intergovernmental meetings of experts, seminars and workshops in which both government representatives and businessmen take part. In such meetings and various studies, the lack of suitably trained managerial personnel has been frequently identified as impeding the establishment of joint ventures and their effective operation in the countries of central and eastern Europe.

The Entrepreneurship and Management Development Branch of the Department for Enterprise and Cooperation Development of the International Labour Organisation (ILO), has also closely monitored and emphasised in its studies and programmes the central issue of the lack of management expertise in economies in transition as one of the major problems and impediments to structural reforms.

Given the particular interest of the ECE in the subject of foreign direct investment and of the ILO in management development, our respective organizations decided to cooperate in the preparation of this Guide on "Management Development in East-West Joint Ventures". It is intended primarily for companies establishing business ventures in central and eastern Europe and for management training specialists in both eastern and western countries. It will also be of interest to governmental officials responsible for promoting enterprise and management development in their respective countries.

Acknowledgements are due to Mr. Geoffrey Hamilton of the United Nations Economic Commission for Europe, as author, and to Mr. Joseph Prokopenko of the Entrepreneurship and Management Development Branch of the ILO for both his editorial advice and comments on sections dealing with management development and training. Ms. Dominique Rames of the ECE assisted with the presentation and typing of the Guide.

Norman Scott
Director
Trade Division
United Nations Economic
Commission for Europe

Philip Neck
Chief
Entrepreneurship and Management
Development Branch Enterprise and
Co-operative Development Department
International Labour Organisation

INTRODUCTION

Scope of the problem

A key issue facing western companies active in eastern European countries[1] or planning operations there is the recruitment of qualified management, both expatriate and local. This situation arises from the scarcity or lack in the "economies in transition" of:

- management personnel with experience of the operation of market economies;

- management training institutions in eastern Europe, their limited financial resources and the shortage of qualified trainers;

- associations of management development professionals which could promote management training and provide a source of quality control for the large number of new, market-oriented management schools which have been established in the region in recent years;

- experience of western management schools with eastern Europe and their lack of any tailor-made, teaching models for these countries;

- knowledge, particularly amongst western firms, about available management skills in these countries and their suitability for the new requirements;

- financial resources available in these countries to fund training programmes.

Figures showing both the extent to which joint ventures have become operational in eastern Europe and their rate of increase illustrate both the scale of the management problem facing enterprises and the need to find solutions. By the end of September 1992, there were approximately 52,800 joint ventures registered in these countries, distributed as follows:

---

[1]   The term "eastern Europe" is used for the sake of brevity and as employed in the Guide refers to Albania, Bulgaria, the Commonwealth of Independent States, the Czech and Slovak Republics, Estonia, Hungary, Latvia, Lithuania, Poland and Romania which are currently in transition from a centrally planned to a market economy. The terms "economies in transition" and "eastern European countries" should be understood here as referring to the same group of countries.

Table 1

Number of Foreign Investment and Joint Ventures
Registered in Economies in Transition, up to 1 October 1992

Countries	Number of Joint Venture Projects
Bulgaria	1,100
Hungary	12,110
C.I.S.	9,100
Czechoslovakia	5,100
Poland	9,000
Romania	16,259

<u>Source</u>: ECE East-West Joint Ventures Database.

However, in all of these countries - with the exception of Hungary - over half of these joint ventures were not operational. (In the former Soviet Union, for example, less than 40 per cent of registered joint ventures were operational). It is probable that difficulties in finding and training suitably qualified managers have played a role in impeding the speedy and effective implantation of joint ventures in these economies.

Despite the difficulties in starting up, the rate at which joint ventures are being registered is nevertheless impressive. In some countries last year the number of joint ventures doubled. If last year's rate of increase is maintained then by the end of 1993, there could be around 80,000 joint ventures registered in eastern Europe. Such an increase would create an even bigger demand for managerial personnel and thereby accentuate the difficulties these enterprises face in establishing their operations in these countries.

The problem facing joint ventures in eastern Europe is not only one of finding suitably qualified managers to run them. It also involves the problem of marrying different management cultures into an integrated business organization with the best possible chance to succeed. Operating issues in any joint venture are difficult to manage. Even in joint ventures between western partners they pose difficulties. East-West joint ventures will be more difficult to manage effectively since the partners have a different cultural heritage and a scant base of shared management knowledge. Some of the differences in values, culture and behaviour between managers from the West and from the East are laid out in Box 1.

BOX 1 DIFFERENCES IN VALUE SYSTEMS BETWEEN MANAGEMENT FROM EAST AND WEST		
	WEST	**EAST**
Importance Attached	Wealth Informality and Competence	Equity Protocol, Rank and Status
Emphasis on Motivation	Individualism	Group Unity
Education as investment	Personal Development, Success	Prestige
Dealing with Conflicts	Creative Energy to be managed	To be avoided
Approach to Output	Quality, Sales, Marketing	Production, Quantity
Communication	Horizontal/Vertical, Open, Networking	Vertical, Closed
Responsibility/Risks	Looking to take Risks	To be avoided

Source: J. Prokopenko, "Human Resources Management in Economies in Transition: The East European Case", MAN DEV/66, ILO, 1992.

Few western and eastern managers have experience with each other's systems and as a result, they are likely to hold distorted views of the other. It is of crucial importance that western managers who are to be involved in joint venture operations realize that systems in eastern European countries, while presently in great flux, if not upheaval, have their own management culture which has evolved from deeply rooted traditions, values, and priorities. This inherited management culture needs to be understood and respected by Western managers even though it may be completely unfamiliar.

Background to the guide

One of the proposals made at a Workshop on "Management of East-West Joint Ventures" organized by the ECE and the Austrian Federal Economic Chamber in the spring of 1991, was for assistance and coordinated action by appropriate international agencies to provide, regular up-to-date information on:

- government funding (at the multilateral and bilateral levels) to assist in the costs of management training in eastern Europe;
- availability of management development and training courses in western and eastern Europe;
- various training approaches to the management problem, so that enterprises might be advised on how to make the best use of their funds.

The ILO has also received a number of similar requests from its constituents - governments and employers' organizations - on similar issues as well as direct requests for advisory services and information on management development, strategies, approaches, methods and techniques, and institutional mechanisms to be promoted in East European countries.

In the light of these requests the Economic Commission for Europe and the Entrepreneurship and Management Development Branch of the ILO have produced this Guide. A pre-publication version of this Guide was discussed at a Workshop at the Italian Institute of Foreign Trade, Rome, Italy, in July 1992.

The Guide is divided into six sections:

1. the setting - describes the growth of foreign direct investment and the road to a market economy in eastern Europe;

2. examines management practices in the economies in transition;

3. describes the management requirements for East-West joint ventures and foreign investment projects and western company responses;

4. discusses the role of the management training institutions in East and West and provides information on courses currently being provided to train managers from eastern Europe;

5. outlines the financial support available for enterprises establishing businesses in eastern Europe to train managers;

6. provides useful information, addresses, bibliographies on the topic.

1. MARKETIZATION OF THE ECONOMY AND THE GROWTH OF FOREIGN DIRECT INVESTMENT

1.1 THE ROAD TO A MARKET ECONOMY

The growing interest of western firms in establishing activities in central and eastern Europe is principally due to the transformation of the countries of the region from centrally planned to market economies. All the countries of the region, some as part of shock therapy and others through a slower, but equally comprehensive programme of structural adjustment have begun to introduce the components of a new economic framework and as a result, a new form of management. The main components of this new economic framework include the following:

Property rights reform

Many of the Governments in eastern Europe have introduced new constitutional arrangements guaranteeing private property and committing themselves to provide fair compensation for any assets nationalized in the future. The establishment of clear property rights and an environment conducive to enforcing them are essential ingredients of moving towards market-based economic systems.

Macroeconomic stabilization

The Governments have also introduced stabilization programmes to curb inflation and eliminate the large overhang that had been created in the economy as a result of excess money and credit creation and subsidized prices. A sound fiscal policy has been aimed at achieving a more or less balanced budget; monetary policy has aimed at imposing tight credit conditions and limiting monetary growth; while prices have been liberalized and economic activities deregulated. Several countries further have introduced wage ceilings to avoid a wage-price spiral.

The results, to date, of these policies have varied widely between countries. Some, like the Czech and Slovak Republics have made considerable progress in stabilizing their economies. Others have been less successful particularly with regard to reducing their budget deficits. As output and demand have both fallen in the economies in transition, so the yield from the taxation of state-owned enterprises has been reduced, while expenditures particularly on social security have tended to rise. Moreover, the collection of taxes from companies in the emerging private sector has proved more difficult than expected. Consequently, many countries have failed to achieve the deficit targets which the IMF had set as a condition for the disbursal of its loans.

Price liberalization

To end the system of administered and controlled prices, Governments of eastern Europe have pursued a policy of price liberalization. In Poland, Bulgaria and the former Czech and Slovak Federal Republic, this policy was done almost overnight: 75% of prices were freed instantaneously. In Hungary and Romania price liberalization has proceeded more slowly. By 1992, in the former Czech and Slovak Federal Republic 95% of all prices had been freed. In this way, the price mechanism as the coordinator of economic decision is being introduced.

Predictably, price liberalization gave a sharp boost to inflation. The initial price burst in Russia, for example, where in the early months of 1992 about 80 per cent of wholesale and 90 per cent of retail prices had been freed from central control, raised them by some 650 per cent from their December 1991 levels. Although here as in other countries inflation rates have come down, they still remain high, particularly in the CIS countries.

Trade and foreign exchange liberalization

To counter the scope for monopolistic price increases for domestic suppliers in situations where prices are being liberalized, Governments have fostered trade and foreign exchange liberalization thereby providing their economies with "correct" market signals from abroad and injecting some competition. This has involved dismantling the highly restrictive trade regimes e.g. export and import quotas, licensing system and barriers to trade which had been erected under the previous system and their replacement by more conventional trade policy instruments, e.g. tariffs and exchange rates.

Although such measures are necessary to protect infant and traditional industries, certain governments - the former Czech and Slovak Federal Republic, Hungary and Poland - have been swift to reduce these barriers and have adopted comparatively uniform and low tariffs. They have also reformed their exchange rate system, doing away with the previous system of multiple rates and creating one based on a single exchange rate. To date, most of the countries have been sensitive to the threat of inflation and have used their exchange rate in an effort to keep this under control.

Enterprise restructuring

In all transition economies enterprises restructuring is urgently needed. In these countries, products and production technologies are years behind internationally competitive standards. Production of goods in eastern Europe led to the wasteful use of resources (demonstrated by data showing that the intensity of capital, labour and material use is typically much greater than in market economies at roughly comparable development levels). Furthermore, the inherited industrial organization is ill-suited to the requirements of a modern, internationally-competitive production structure. Enterprises are typically much too large and much too autarchic. Under central planning, production was constrained not by the extent of the demands of the market or the availability of finance, but by the availability of inputs, including capital and labour. The main features which were responsible for producing such a system were the absence of competition, automatic cost-plus pricing, the use of soft budgets which irrespective of their performance kept producers afloat and the authorities' preference for dealing with a small number of large firms.

For a number of reasons enterprise restructuring is proving particularly difficult to achieve: there is a lack of personnel with the necessary know-how; a lack of new sources of credit; soaring debt between enterprises; a poor basic information about business; and an uncertain business environment; as well as bureaucratic and political resistance.

Current-Account convertibility

Convertibility and a functioning market for foreign exchange are important ingredients of a market economy. Rather than attempting to achieve full convertibility on current and capital account - where foreign exchange is available without any restriction - the former Czech and Slovak Federal Republic, Estonia, Hungary, Poland and Slovenia have achieved only current-account convertibility. This level of convertibility, which secures foreign exchange for export/import transactions also permits the repatriation of profits earned by foreign enterprises in local currencies and is thus highly attractive to foreign firms.

Achieving internal convertibility for the other economies in transition has proved more problematic. In Russia, the Government announced that the rouble would be made internally convertible on 1 July 1992; but strong downward pressure on the rouble made worse by the very low level of international reserves of hard currency, forced the Government to switch to a limited rouble convertibility with a greatly undervalued exchange rate. Likewise, in Romania, in November 1991, the Government attempted to introduce internal convertibility, in spite of the extremely low level of its hard currency reserves. In the absence of sufficient currency inflows, banks were soon forced with a severe shortage of foreign exchange and were obliged in early 1992 to ration foreign exchange thereby in effect suspending internal convertibility.

Labour market reforms

In centrally planned economies, every adult of working age was guaranteed a job and a salary. Wage differences were narrow, and were unrelated to skill and productivity. Accordingly, effectively functioning labour markets are being created by Governments so that wages are tailored to effort and results and job security becomes related to economic factors.

Of particular importance, in view of the unemployment that will result as a consequence of these reforms, is the creation and funding of a social safety net. One legacy of the old system is the almost complete absence of a social safety net, including its most important feature, unemployment compensation for workers. Governments have tried to make the necessary social safety net arrangements prior to the implementation of their programmes of large scale privatization although doubts remain as to whether their untested means will prove strong enough to stand the enormous strain. For example, according to an ILO study of 500 Russian factories, at the end of December 1991, there were 7,000 people registered as unemployed, but only 600 were receiving benefits.

Privatization of state-owned corporations

All Governments have recognized the need to shift ownerships of the majority of state assets to the private sector. The important goal is to transform ownership so that managers act according to market conditions and signals. Programmes adopted in individual countries combine, in most cases, traditional techniques of market-based privatization in the form of public auctions, market offerings and direct sales, with some measure of free distribution in the form of vouchers, coupons or certificates of various degrees of transferability. The two extreme variants are being applied in the Czech and Slovak Republics, with a massive distribution of vouchers to the population at large, and in Hungary, where no free distribution is envisaged. Although small-scale privatization -shops, restaurants etc. - has proceeded quickly in Hungary and the former Czech and Slovak Federal Republic and Poland as well but to a lesser degree in Bulgaria and Romania, far less progress has been made with large-scale privatization. Problems of valuation, defining ownership of assets, creating effective mechanisms for selling where capital markets are either in their infancy or non-existent and growing political objections to foreigners acquiring corporate assets and land explain the slowness of the process, although the initial plans for selling off these enterprises were extremely ambitious.

Nevertheless, after some delays, the pace of privatization in certain eastern European countries looks set to accelerate dramatically. In early spring of 1993, millions of Czech and Slovak citizens and several hundred investment privatization funds will become shareholders of 1491 Czech and Slovak companies. On 14 May 1992 when a list of these companies was made available, the total book value of their shares was estimated to be 299,4 bn Korunas, or USD 10.4 bn.

New foreign investment regimes

The majority of the economies in transition have placed a high priority in attracting foreign direct investment (FDI) to assist them in their transition process. Consequently, the legislative framework has been rapidly liberalized to allow:

- full foreign ownership of corporate assets. Only in Albania does the foreign investment law not expressly stipulate that a foreign firm can fully own corporate assets.

- easier entry procedures. In most countries, foreign firms do not require Government approval to set up business ventures.

- few industries and sectors are closed to foreign companies.

- fiscal incentives to foreign investors, their size depending on the importance of the investment to the host economy.

- profit repatriation. Foreign enterprises can repatriate profits earned in local and convertible currencies in Estonia, Hungary, Poland, the former Czech and Slovak Federal Republic and Slovenia and with some restrictions in Bulgaria and Romania. The lack of convertible currency in other economies in transition forces western enterprises in these countries to use barter arrangements or foreign exchange auctions.

There is thus a growing understanding among eastern European countries that FDI regimes must be so created as to provide good business conditions for foreign corporations.

1.2   EAST-WEST JOINT VENTURES - THE RECENT DEVELOPMENTS

Summary of recent trends

● The rate at which new joint ventures and FDI projects are being registered is continuing to accelerate in Hungary, Poland, Czech and Slovak Republics and Romania. New FDI projects continue also to increase in the CIS: since October 1991 a further 1,700 projects have been registered.

● Western companies, which in the past were required to establish joint ventures with local firms, are increasingly building new, greenfield plants or taking over privatized state companies. In Hungary in 1991 over two-thirds of foreign capital was attracted into the country through the acquisition of local firms. In Poland by the first half of 1992, foreign firms had acquired stakes in 1340 enterprises.

● The impact of foreign direct investment on most of the economies of central and eastern Europe continues to be small. In the CIS according to estimates only around 40 per cent of joint ventures are operational. In contrast Hungary where the bulk of FDI projects are operational has attracted a cumulative total of USD 3 bn, and a capital inflow for 1991 equivalent to more than 5% of Gross Domestic Product (GDP). This capital inflow has allowed the Government to build up its foreign exchange reserves and ease the country's balance of payments.

● The preferred activity of foreign firms in eastern Europe is manufacturing (accounting for between 40 and 50 per cent of all activities) and services. Few projects have been begun in the regions potentially lucrative mining, oil and gas industries.

● The availability of highly educated research and scientific workers which are significantly cheaper than the West has encouraged some western enterprises to establish R&D centres in the East. GE for examples has shifted four of its nine lighting research centres to Tungsram, its Hungarian light-bulb making subsidiary.

● Most projects remain small. Despite newspaper headlines, the vast majority of investments in eastern Europe, as measured by the size of the foreign contribution to the initial capitalization are below USD 500 thousand.

● Most of eastern Europe's foreign investors come from the developed market economies of western Europe - with Germany, Austria, Italy, France, Switzerland, United Kingdom, Sweden and the Netherlands being the most prominent. Much less interest has been shown by the world's two largest investing nations - the USA and Japan.

Scope

Overall, by 1 October 1992 there were 52,800 FDI projects registered in the countries of central and eastern Europe (CIS, Hungary, Poland, the former Czech and Slovak Federal Republic, Bulgaria, Romania, Estonia, Latvia and Lithuania). At the beginning of 1991 there had been around 15,000 FDI projects registered. The growth in FDI projects has been particularly marked in Hungary, Romania, the former Czech and Slovak Federal Republic and Poland. The CIS too despite political uncertainties has continued to attract new FDI projects; Bulgaria in contrast has not succeeded in attracting the same level of investor interest from abroad as the other economies in transition.

Capitalization

By totalling the foreign components to the initial statutory capital of registered FDI projects, it can be estimated that by 1 October 1992 the total value of foreign investment in the former Czech and Slovak Federal Republic, Hungary, the former USSR, Poland, Romania and Bulgaria amounted to USD 12.4 bn. This sum represents less than 1 per cent of the value of the world stock of FDI abroad, estimated in 1990 to be USD 1500 bn. By means of further comparison, the total inward flow of foreign investment to developing countries was USD 28 bn for 1991 and to central and eastern Europe for the same year around USD 4 bn.

In their difficult economic circumstances the effect of the transfer of capital of this magnitude would assist these countries' balance of payments and improve conditions for macroeconomic stability. However, the figure of USD 12.4 bn has to be qualified in several respects. First, many projects which are registered fail to become operational and thus the capital is never actually transferred into the country. Second, in some countries the bulk of western capital contribution to FDI projects comes in the form of transfer of machinery and equipment, know-how, patents, market access, etc. rather than hard-currency cash contributions.

Average size of FDI project

Most foreign direct investment projects in eastern Europe are small or very small. In the CIS in more than 75 per cent of all joint ventures, the foreign capital invested was less than USD 1 million. In Hungary the average foreign capital contribution was USD 600 thousand; in Poland USD 130 thousand and in Romania around USD 10-20 thousand. The comparatively small size of FDI projects can be explained by several factors. First many are involved in the provision of a variety of services which do not require a large initial capitalization. Second, negotiation on many large-scale projects in capital intensive industries - oil, petro-chemical, metallurgy - particularly in the CIS continues to be stalled as a result of red tape. Third in view of the legal uncertainties and overall economic conditions, western corporations are keen to minimize the risk by putting in as little capital as possible.

Countries of origin

Overall the main investing nations in eastern European are those countries with close geographical and trading links with the region (see Table 2). Among corporations from the EC, German enterprises have the largest share in the respective eastern countries (particularly Poland, the CIS and the former Czech and Slovak Federal Republic) followed by Italy (particularly in Hungary, Romania) and the USA and the United Kingdom. Of EFTA countries, Austrian companies account for a major share of all registered ventures (particularly in Hungary, Czech and Slovak Republics) followed by Sweden (particularly in Poland and the Baltic States) and Finland (especially in the CIS and Estonia).

Table 2

Principal Investing Countries in Selected Economies in Transition

	Top five countries (by number of ventures)		Top five countries (by value in millions USD)	
Former Czech and Slovak Federal Republic */	Austria	(80)	- */	
	Germany	(56)	Germany	(467.2)
	Switzerland	(16)	U.S.A.	(64.0)
	Italy	(9)	Austria	(51.2)
	United Kingdom,)		Belgium	(32)
	Netherlands and)	(7)	France	(16)
	France)			
Hungary	Austria	(57)	Austria	(200.9)
	Germany	(252)	U.S.A.	(91.6)
	U.S.A.	(62)	Germany	(78.6)
	Italy	(46)	Luxembourg	(54.5)
Poland */	Germany	(1686)	Germany	(160.8)
	U.S.A.	(514)	U.S.A.	(113.2)
	Sweden	(396)	Netherlands	(80.6)
	Austria	(380)	France	(83.2)
	Netherlands	(346)	United Kingdom	(53.6)
Former Soviet Union	Germany	(281)	U.S.A.	(360.2)
	U.S.A.	(247)	Finland	(356.9)
	Finland	(183)	Germany	(346.1)
	Italy	(130)	France	(181.2)
	Austria	(115)		
Romania	Germany	(1711)	France	(54.7)
	Italy	(1304)	Germany	(54.3)
	Turkey	(1317)	United Kingdom	(52.5)
	Syria	(1199)	U.S.A.	(44.1)
	China	(719)	Italy	(19.7)

Source: ECE East-West Joint Ventures Database.

*/ In the former Czech and Slovak Federal Republic, the top 5 investing countries by value refers only to foreign inward investment for 1991.

US corporations are active in Hungary, Poland and the CIS. Japan, however, does not figure among the top 5 investing nations anywhere in central and eastern Europe. Traditionally Japanese firms are less attracted by cheap labour as an incentive to establish production in a particular country (Japanese companies instead prefer to use high technology production processes, robotics, etc.). In addition the lack of purchasing power for their higher value products in eastern Europe is another reason for this current lack of interest.

Distribution of FDI projects by industrial activity

FDI projects in eastern Europe have covered a wide number of industries and sectors but overall they have tended to concentrate on the following: bulk chemicals; food processing and packaging; construction; hotels, consumer goods; assembly of personal computers; and automobiles.

Chemicals. Projects in the chemicals industry are often sizeable and found in the CIS. Such projects in the latter include Du Pont de Nemours (USA), Dow Chemicals (USA), Feruzzi (Italy) and ICI (United Kingdom). The western corporations are attracted to investing in chemical production by the ample supply of cheap natural gas, oil and other chemical raw materials. In addition they see significant opportunities in moving into the production of higher value added products such as plastics synthetic fibres, paints, etc.

In pharmaceuticals, Sanofi (France) has established a joint venture with Chinoin (Hungary), but in general the absence of patent protection in these countries' domestic legislation has to date limited inward foreign investment in this branch of the chemicals industry.

Power generating equipment industry. The strong demand for energy produced in a more cost effective and environmentally friendly manner, the existence of low cost but highly skilled workforces and the need to be locally based in order to win public contracts to build new power plants, have encouraged many of the West's leading power generating equipment manufacturers to invest heavily in the region. For example, Siemens (Germany) took over the turbine generator arm of Skoda in the former Czech and Slovak Federal Republic and Madrina (Germany) has acquired a 30 per cent stake in Elektrosila of Russia to produce electricity generating and power equipment. Also, over the last three years Asea Brown Boveri, the Swiss-Swedish company, has concluded over 26 joint ventures in eastern Europe, including several in Poland where its main company, ABB-Zemach employs more than 50 per cent of the 16,000 people now working for the company's joint ventures in eastern Europe.

Oil. It had always been expected that the CIS's vast, underexploited oil deposits would be a major source of attraction for large western oil companies but problems with financing and red tape have led to endless delays. Recently, however a number of very large deals have been concluded: Conoco (USA) has agreed a USD 3 bn venture with the Russian authorities to develop close to the Polar Circle, the Dosyuchevskoye, Ardalinskoye and Kolvinskoye Oil Fields in the North East Urals; Total (France) has agreed another large project in Russia to develop four oil fields located in the Republic of Komi and a smaller one in the same Republic to develop the Romashkino deposit in Tataria; and Elf-Aquitaine (France) has begun exploration in the Aktiubinsk Oil Field in Kazakhstan and the Saratov-Volgograd Oil Field in Russia.

In addition, several ventures have been concluded in downstream activities, like oil refining. For example, Conoco has agreed to invest USD 1 bn over a number of years to modernize and expand the Gdansk Oil Refinery in Poland.

Food processing and packaging. With chronic food shortages, particularly of quality food, the potential in this area is significant for western firms and already many FDI projects have begun. The greatest scope lies in projects which introduce superior packaging technologies and cut down on food waste because of poor processing, transport and/or storage. Hence, Tetra-Pak (Sweden) has established joint ventures to produce food-packaging materials, and APV (United Kingdom) is constructing food processing machinery in the CIS. In addition, D'Agard (France) a refrigeration construction firm is setting up an ice-cream factory in Poland and Allied Lyons (United Kingdom) is building the same type of factory in Russia.

Construction. This industry is attracting investment because of the strong demand for superior works and high quality materials and the overall requirement in eastern Europe to improve the region's physical infrastructure. In other cases, FDIs in this sector are taking advantage of opportunities to build hotels for western tourists, office buildings and housing for western businessmen and even participate in the construction of new plants for some of the FDI projects in manufacturing . Examples include: in the housing/building sector, Otis Elevators (USA) has established two joint ventures in the CIS; John Brown of the United Kingdom has established a joint venture with a Slovenian company to construct a factory in the Russian Federation; Kone has created ventures in Hungary and Poland; Schindler (Switzerland) has a joint venture in the CIS; Bau Holding (Austria) is active in the construction industry in Hungary; and there are also several projects in the glass industry -Pilkington (United Kingdom) in Poland and Guardian (USA) in Hungary.

Consumer goods industry. The manufacturing of low priced consumer goods - detergents, chocolates, foods, cigarettes in eastern Europe is attracting numerous investments: Nestlé (Switzerland) and, BSN (France) together acquired Cokoladovny of the former Czech and Slovak Federal Republic; BAT (United Kingdom) has a joint venture with Pecs (Hungary) to manufacture cigarettes, Philip Morris has acquired stakes in the Czech Tabak company and in the Hungarian tobacco firm, Egri Dohanygyar and R.J. Reynolds (USA) has acquired a controlling stake in a new company, RJR-Petro, to produce cigarettes for the Russian market. Unilever (Anglo/Dutch) has with Ferruzi (Italy) taken controlling stakes in several Hungarian sugar factories and has begun to manufacture detergents and soap in Poland; Proctor and Gamble (USA) has acquired Rakona a soap and detergents manufacturer in the former Czech and Slovak Federal Republic; Sara Lee (USA) has a venture with Compack of Hungary in the food industry and United Biscuits of the United Kingdom has acquired a controlling stake in Gyori Kekaz of Hungary.

The assembly of personal computers and software development. The restrictions placed on the export of strategic materials imposed by the Coordinating Committee for Multilateral Export Controls (CoCom) prevented until recently the export of even low-powered PCs to eastern Europe. Only able to use this less powerful machinery, eastern European programmers became highly adept at solving complex tasks and in developing a variety of software for that purpose. This has created both a huge pent-up demand for PCs in eastern Europe (in the CIS there are estimated to be only 500,000 PCs) and a highly skilled workforce of computer programmers.

Thus, numerous FDI projects have been established. In the CIS for example, this branch of activity was the most favoured by foreign enterprises. Large enterprises such as ICL, DEC, IBM and Olivetti are positioning themselves in eastern Europe to exploit this market. In April 1992, IBM took a majority stake in a subsidiary of Muszertechnika, the privately owned Hungarian computer distributor and manufacturers which has 25 per cent share of the Hungarian market.

Car and truck industry. Among European car producers Volkswagen (Germany) has taken the lead in this industry by its investments in Skoda the biggest producer of cars in the region and the small Slovak producer Baz in the former Czech and Slovak Federal Republic. Fiat (Italy) is next with its long-term investments in the CIS and in Poland, followed by Renault which has a plant also in Poland.

GM has taken the lead among US producers in eastern and central Europe with its "greenfield" (first time) investment at Szentgotthard, Hungary. Ford also, has signed an agreement to supply diesel engines to the Hungarian market.

Japanese producers so far are poorly represented with only Suzuki having invested in a manufacturing venture - Magjar, Suzuki- in Hungary in a collaborative deal which involved C. Itoh and the International Finance Corporation. In the main Japanese car manufactures have restricted their activities to the setting-up of sales offices in eastern Europe.

In the truck industry, Mercedes Benz (Germany) has established a joint venture with two firms, Liaz and Avia (Former Czech and Slovak Federal Republic) and Volvo has negotiated a joint venture with Jelcz (Poland).

Related investments by car component manufacturers include: Pirelli's (Italy) production of tyres in the CIS; Trempex's (Sweden/France) investment in Estonia to produce car wind shields; the acquisition by T & N, the United Kingdom components manufacturer, of Osinek the sole Czech producer of automotive brake and fraction products; and the joint venture of Cubot International of the USA to produce materials for car type manufacturing in the Czech Republic.

Hotels. The growing demand for hotel rooms by western business and tourists, the high room rates in hotels, the 100% guaranteed occupancy rate, and the income from allowing other services to operate in the premises e.g. rent-a-car firms has attracted numerous FDI projects in this industry. Typically these offer the investor substantial hard-currency cash flows with rapid recovery of initial investment. Acquisition of hotel sites remains, however, a problem in many countries because of problems in securing titles to land. Nevertheless, Hilton (USA), and Mövenpick (Switzerland) have established hotels in Hungary; Oberoi (India) has acquired a stake in Hungar hotels; and the Compagnie Générale de Bâtiment et Construction (CGD) (France) has invested USD 140 millions in the construction of the Hotel *Atrium* in Prague.

2. MANAGEMENT PRACTICE IN EASTERN EUROPE PRIOR TO MARKETIZATION

In many cases the lack of suitably qualified managers in eastern Europe has invariably been explained by the central planning system which operated in all the countries of the region until recently. Although central planning has utterly collapsed, management culture and practice will remain for some time and therefore it is important for western managers to understand some of its basic features to appreciate the nature of management in eastern Europe and the ways to change it.

2.1. MANAGEMENT UNDER CENTRAL PLANNING

The centralized or "directive-planning" system was born during the period of the first five-year plan in the Soviet Union, around 1929-1932. The efforts to fulfil overambitious plans, complicated by the consequences of resistance to collectivisation, led to acute shortages throughout the economy. To impose the priorities of industrialization and rapid economic growth and to ensure that key projects received necessary materials and equipment, centralized system of production planning and supply allocation was set up. This planning system became the essential characteristic of Soviet-type centrally controlled planned economies. The market was viewed as being too inefficient and slow to carry out the plans to transform a backward country at breakneck speed. The same motivation - to overcome severe shortages in the economy - led several eastern European countries to adopt a replica of the Soviet model of central planning in the years after World War II.

Under traditional central planning the typical Soviet enterprise was a state-owned plant operating on the principle of one-man responsibility and control by a director or manager appointed by the state (usually by the Party). Through a system of vertical coordination and control, central planners issued directives down a chain of command to each production unit on what to produce and how to meet requirements. This emphasis on "vertical connections" in the economy reflected an effort by the planners to reduce their dependence on the "horizontal connections" (i.e. spontaneous immediate contacts emerging between economic units). The enterprise thus participated vertically in the planning process, responding to the downward flowing "control figures" (broad outline features of the central plan). The State Planning Commission, *Gosplan* received general instructions from the Party/State apparatus together with data/requests from lower echelons of the economic hierarchy and used the technique known as Material Balances (computations of the supply of and demand for products) to formulate the "control figures". Once the plan had been approved, the principal function of the industrial enterprise became the fulfilment of its plans (technical, industrial and financial) broken down into annual, quarterly and monthly targets.

This Soviet model of central planning appears to cast management in the role of simple executants of orders. They were told what to produce, from whom to obtain inputs; they had no control over prices, nor could they exceed the prescribed wage and salary bill. Orders which managers had to obey poured down from above on a variety of topics. This picture suggested that essentially managers were there to supervise technical operations. If one adds to this that certain decisions(e.g. over dismissals, welfare funds, etc.) required the consent of the trade union and that they were subject to the supervisory role of the Party and of several other controlling and checking agencies, not to mention the bank, the managers' standing and importance within this economic system appeared even smaller.

However it would be wrong to assume that managers were relegated under central planning to such an insignificant role. Managerial powers *de facto* arose in centrally planned economies from the following circumstances:

(a)   In practice it was impossible for the central planners to take the bulk of detailed decisions and to communicate the requirements to the enterprise management in a suitably desegregated way. To take one example: it was not enough for industrial planners to issue a command for "agricultural machinery" to the production units; there had to be a distinction between different kinds of combined-harvesters, harrows, ploughs, cultivators, milking machines and so on. In addition, the productive process always involved what had to be provided by other enterprises. Central planners could not deal with all the information required in this huge task so that much power was *de facto* decentralized to the level of the firm.

(b)   Both output plans and inputs, though decided above, were often implemented on the basis of information and proposals submitted by management. This is what one commentator described as "commands written by the recipients". Even when as often happened, the actual/plan order differed from what was proposed, it was still influenced by management "on the ground" which knew best what the plant was capable of doing.[2]

(c)   A variety of innovations, in product design and production methods could potentially be initiated at the enterprise level, and so the use of incentives for management (and disincentives) were of utmost importance.

(d)   Because of what was termed "centralized pluralism" - instructions coming from both the planners and the Ministries - orders which reached the management from different quarters of the State apparatus, could be contradictory or mutually exclusive. In these instances, managers had some choice thrust upon them as to which order to obey.

(e)   Particularly in matters relating to the supply of inputs, there was much scope for semi-legal (or even downright illegal) initiatives. Indeed a good deal depended on a whole network of informal links, which supplemented the official hierarchy and channels.

While the scope for management to develop its powers was enhanced under this system, the overall features of centrally planned economies nevertheless restricted managers in eastern Europe from emulating the status and authority of their counterparts in the West.

---

[2] This provided an excellent opportunity for enterprises to suggest "plans" well below their actual resources.

These features included:

(1)   No common standard of value to judge the performance of an enterprise.   Instead of a single objective indicator of an enterprise's success (such as profit in the market economy) the centrally planning authorities typically used multiple "success indicators".   They included at various stages: gross output (val.); net output; output in physical terms using various units of measurement: light, weight, numbers, and length; labour utilization; cost reduction; and profit (as a percentage of costs, as opposed to capital).   The result was a mass of increasingly changing and often inconsistent indicators that had the effect of restricting management efficiency.   For example, using the tonnage of metal goods produced as an indicator, managers were encouraged to fulfil the plan by manufacturing <u>heavy</u> and more expensive goods when lighter materials would have been more economical.

(2)   No rational system of incentives and rewards.   The lack of any common indicator for enterprise performance made it very difficult to offer managers any rational system of incentives. Payments to incentive funds for managers could be calculated on the basis of: an increase in sales; increase in profits, and could be conditional on fulfilment of other elements of the plan e.g. delivery success, increased labour productivity and so on.   They were paid into a number of incentive funds e.g. material incentive, housing fund, investment fund and then out to the manager using bewilderingly complicated formulae.

(3)   The estrangement of the producers from the customers.   Unlike in market economies, enterprises were not responding to customer preferences.   They had no direct links with retail units and no experience of customer dissatisfaction with their products.   Where enterprise performance was judged solely on output, then output only had to be produced, not sold.   Hence there was an in-built neglect of customer needs, and qualitative aspects of production, especially in low-priority sectors concerned with heterogeneous output (textiles, for example).   This helps explain the paradox of increasing stockpiles of poor-quality products in a situation of general consumer goods scarcity.

(4)   The incentive system as a disincentive to efficient production.   Discontinuous incentives operated as part of a system where there was a sharp line of demarcation between success and failure.   Incentives systems were designed to offer rewards if the plans were fulfilled 100 per cent (particularly, the physical output plan); failure was defined as falling short of the established quotas.   The tendency for a director to aim for a "slack" plan (one which calls for less than feasible output) revolved around the incentive system, which involved no bonuses for less than 100 per cent fulfilment and led to the tendency of managers to understate their productive capacity.   The all-or-nothing philosophy of the incentive system encouraged: simulation -wilful misclassification of commodities to show favourable results; storming - regular seasonal sprints on production to fulfil the quota; and hoarding, which occurred to facilitate plan fulfilment in subsequent periods.

(5)   Creation of a seller's market.   The centrally planned economy gave birth to what economists call a "seller's market".   Under these circumstances, selling presents few difficulties for the producer, since the high deficit pressure under which the economy operates means that there is a chronic shortage of goods and sellers have little trouble disposing of whatever they produce. This creates no competition in the economy between producers even those selling even the same goods.   Thus, centrally planned economies allowed no room for the innovating entrepreneur and the creative manager.

2.2 THE PRINCIPAL WEAKNESSES IN EASTERN EUROPEAN MANAGEMENT

While some managers from eastern Europe possessed some basic knowledge of the fundamentals of market economies - profit, competition, price, etc. - there was a lack of understanding about what these concepts meant in practice: e.g. the function of profits, the reasons for pricing goods, the importance for an enterprise of developing its comparative advantage, etc. Companies in eastern Europe had different objectives than in the West: They fulfilled the plans fixed by the Central Planning Authorities; the making of a profit was strictly secondary to this primary goal.

Limited training. As a result, eastern managers had no training in how to run an enterprise in a competitive environment. Their formal education had equipped them to run enterprises solely in a centrally-planned economy. The skills which they were taught were task-specific and of a technical and functional nature more in line with their basic education which was typically in engineering. The knowledge which was imparted to them also was in keeping with the rather marginal role they played in the enterprise in comparison to their western counterparts. An enterprise manager, under central planning, had normally no responsibility for such functions as product innovation, budgetary and finance control or human resources development - the responsibility lying with the relevant State ministry. In addition, management especially at senior level, was often entrusted to political appointees who had no formal management education.

The following set of skill shortages is apparent among eastern European managers:

- lack of experience of corporate procedures and methods;
- creativity, initiative and leadership qualities;
- an ability to restructure a business venture (no direct experience in fundamental organizational change);
- accounting, auditing and finance;
- strategic planning;
- marketing;
- human resource management, result-oriented motivation;
- lack of experience of doing business abroad and foreign language skills.

Cost control. The existence of a fixed prices system for manufactured goods meant that managers had no appreciation of the need for cost control. There was no experience in allocating costs to profit centres or assigning responsibility to managers to control cost. In many plants managers used accounting systems just for statistical purposes not to impose any means of cost discipline. The lack of attention to controlling cost resulted in the poorly designed nature of the factory layout, the waste of space and effort and the inefficient management working methods.

Marketing. Managers have no experience in marketing and consequently inadequate skills in product design, distribution, design of brand name, advertising, after-sales service and repair. Western management consultants in visits to large factories in the former Soviet Union to advise on privatization have reported seeing marketing departments consisting of only one person - often an engineer.

International experience. Another feature characteristic of eastern European management was their lack of experience in dealing with businessmen in other countries. The role of the foreign trade organization in the control of the export and import of goods deprived most enterprises in eastern Europe of the possibility to trade. International contacts were confined to a tiny fraction of eastern European business leaders. For example, according to one estimate, less than 5% of factories in the former GDR up to 1990 had any direct trade links with the West. Even with other countries of eastern Europe with a longer history of reform, the situation was similar. For instance, a World Bank study of the directors and managers of Hungary's largest firms showed that only 7% conducted business in other countries. The results of this study are valid for other central and eastern European countries as well. Indeed it was estimated that barely 13% of managers in eastern Europe have ever been in a western country and more than a half only spoke their mother tongue.

Centralized decision-taking. Typically decision-taking within factories in eastern Europe was hierarchical and centralized. Power rested with the Director General of the factory. Middle and lower management merely implemented the decision taken at the top. The authority given to the Director General of the company was also invariably enshrined in the laws of the country. For example the former Law on the Soviet State enterprise explicitly invoked the principle of one person leadership in the administration of enterprises. On the other hand, power over certain issues was devolved to the enterprise's labour collective or the employees' council. In contrast, in market economies the greater variety and the rapid shift in prices, goods and demand requires more day-to-day, flexible decision-taking and hence a more decentralized structure of command. Middle managers have thus much more autonomy and responsibility: they are put in charge of their own profit centres and business units and can decide on new products.

Restructuring. The lack of experience of eastern European managers with restructuring enterprises must also be taken into account. Here again too centralized control in the Ministries, the lack of any price mechanism to determine which products to concentrate and the lack of any market signals to identify consumer preferences meant that managers had no practice in turning companies around as in the West. True, for some time there have been attempts to give enterprises more autonomy from the State and the central planning authorities. Borrowing from western models of management, the authorities have used incentives to encourage managers to become more sensitive to the needs of the customer and to the cost and quality of their product. It is generally recognized, however, that such reforms were not successful in producing more autonomous and market-oriented managers. [3]

Management culture. As a result of the above-mentioned constraints, the present culture of eastern European managers displays some of the following characteristics:

- lack of motivation (managers pay was not based on performance and there was little differential between their income and that of shop floor workers);

- unwillingness to accept responsibility and take charge (the hierarchical structures of central planning discouraged managers in taking initiative even making it a crime under some eastern European legal systems);

- conservative approach to change (it is notable that as a group managers have not been in the forefront of those advocating change in eastern Europe).

---

[3] For a discussion on the limited impact of management reform in Hungary, see, "Hesitating Steps Towards Self-Government in Hungary" by Laszlo Budavari, Economics of Planning, Vol.22, Nos.1-2, 1988.

Adjustment problems

The adjustment by eastern European managers to the new emerging business environment is proving difficult. Not only are managers having to cope with highly unfavourable economic conditions, but also with internal political resistance to the reforms.

Collapse of central planning. In most countries the Ministries which were responsible for providing funds for investment, hard currency, financing and support in raw material purchasing were liquidated and responsibility for these tasks passed to the enterprise. At the same time, the enterprise management is not ready to take over yet. Besides, the market and financial institutions are not in place nor fully operational.

BOX 2

MR. GUROV, GENERAL DIRECTOR OF BOLCHEVICHKA, RUSSIA'S LEADING MEN'S APPAREL MANUFACTURER

Mr. Gurov had trained for five years at the Moscow Institute of Light Industry to be an engineer specialising in the technology of sewn goods. After 10 months as the Technology Manager in the Ministry of Light industry and four years in Bolchevichka as Technical Director, Mr. Gurov was appointed General Director in 1987 at age 34. "Nobody wanted to take this job'. The company was in a very bad position. The former general manager, the sales manager, the chief accountant and his two deputies had all left. The fiscal situation was very poor, plans very demanding, responsibility very high and wages very low." Mr. Gurov had attended a management training course for Soviet managers at Duke University in the US and was also considering MBA and executive programmes in late 1991. He was not a bureaucrat, but a manager sincerely interested in developing his professional managerial training. A man of action, he disliked his bureaucratic year in the Ministry, and he welcomed the challenge that awaited him as General Director of Bolchevichka.

Despite the excitement of increased managerial freedom which has suddenly resulted from the cataclysmic changes, Mr. Gurov was concerned about what he saw as the erosion of social values. Mr. Gurov had thoroughly enjoyed his childhood days in a small community house which his family shared with 12 other families. " I was brought up in a community environment. You see, the relationships we have here in the Soviet Union are quite different from those you have in the West. There, the basic ideology is individualism, and here we have a basic ideology of collectivism. We got used to living in big communities, to deal and to speak and to laugh, and we did not care about the future and the day after tomorrow; we were always sure about the next day. Now we have to transform ourselves into individualists, and that is what I feel sorry about."

Source: The Bolschevichka Apparel Company: Managing in Perestroika by Bill Fischer and George Taucher, 1992 IMD, Lausanne, Switzerland.

Extreme uncertainty. Without the ministries, managers are unsure of to whom they are responsible. There is no longer any explicit system of accountability nor discipline and managers feel uneasy about exercising this new found autonomy. Everywhere there is deep uncertainty over the future of the enterprise and the jobs of its employees (see Box 2 Mr. Gurov). A lot of managers, instead of taking initiatives are just waiting for commands.

Little desire to change. It was often assumed that the new owners or managers once freed from the bureaucratic structures and controls imposed by the system of central planning, would quickly develop new attitudes and methods. However, in many studies on management attitudes to privatization reveal little desire was reported on the part of the managers to change. Their first response to privatization had apparently been to increase wages across-the-board. Little attempt was made to scale-down operating costs. No visible management effort in response to slow growth in sales, in the form of sales promotion, establishing a strong marketing department or decentralizing decision-taking was apparent. The consultants hired to initiate a restructuring programme aimed at cost cutting, establishing a marketing development, personnel evaluations and the development of a new organizational structure, found little response from the management. As one study concluded:

"It is our belief that they (the management) did not see the reason to improve organization and management beyond the point where the implementation of new methods and technique would have threatened traditional managerial behaviours". [4]

---

[4] "Are Polish Managers prepared for the New Era" by G.P. Kasperson and K. Oblo, RFE/Reports, March 1992.

3. MANAGEMENT DEVELOPMENT NEEDS
AND WESTERN RESPONSES

3.1 AN OVERVIEW OF MANAGEMENT DEVELOPMENT NEEDS

East-West joint ventures require numerous types of managers, for various enterprise functions (production, finance, marketing,human resources etc.) and to conduct business at various levels of the organization (senior, middle etc.). Each joint venture has its own specific requirements, depending on the nature and size of its activities and on the corporate styles of the partners concerned. In view of the large number of joint ventures which have been established and given the fact that each of these will have its own specific management requirements, it is only possible to talk in somewhat general terms about management requirements in joint ventures. Nevertheless,we can identify at present two rather broad "types" of joint ventures each of which requires different management skills and personnel.

The first type concerns small-scale, distributing and marketing ventures. The essential purpose of firms which belong to this first category is to market, sell and distribute goods and services. This group can' be further split into two: those whose products and services are destined for the local market - the majority of these firms - and those seeking to export products from eastern mainly to western markets.

Distribution and marketing firms constituted the bulk of those attracted to eastern Europe in the wake of the liberalization of laws on joint ventures in 1987 and 1988. Still relatively few of these joint ventures are involved in full-scale manufacturing.[5]

For joint ventures involved in product based selling activities, management skills in distribution, merchandising, marketing and basic accounting are required. Two types of activities predominate: ensuring that the goods fit the specific requirements of the eastern European market; and that they reach the destinations for which they are intended. For the most part, and given the small size and limited range of their activities, managerial personnel at the middle and junior levels could normally be expected to carry out such tasks.

Service-based operations are varied consisting, for example, of tourism and leisure - e.g. hotels, restaurants, car rentals, etc. - and business services - office accommodation, legal advice, personnel recruitment services and so on. Although the management of a service operation is a practically unknown skill in central and eastern Europe, the expertise required, it might be argued, can be acquired quite easily.

---

[5] See Statistical Survey of Recent Trends in Foreign Investment in the East European Countries Committee on the Development of Trade (Thirty-ninth session, 4-8 December 1990), Economic Commission for Europe.

The second type are <u>large-scale manufacturing joint ventures</u>.This type of joint venture has emerged more recently and is being formed increasingly as a result of the restructuring process affecting state enterprises. Whilst restructuring is taking place in all countries of the region, it is more noticeable in Hungary, Poland and the former Czech and Slovak Federal Republic, that is, those countries where the transition of the economy from a centrally-planned to a market system is more advanced. State-owned enterprises are being restructured as a result of several major reforms involving:

- the dismantling of the central planning system;

- the abolition of the State Trade Organizations and the liberalization of trade;

- the reduction in subsidies and the phasing out of state credits to state-owned enterprises;

- the collapse of the old CMEA trading system;

- the privatization of the state retailing system and of state industrial enterprises.[6]

The essential purpose of the eastern partner in setting up a joint venture is to obtain assistance from the western firm in its restructuring so that it can survive in the more competitive conditions of a market economy. In Hungary joint ventures of this kind have come about for the most part as a consequence of the full or partial privatization of state-owned enterprises. In contrast with the smaller type of joint venture described above, these ventures are active in larger-scale manufacturing activities. Examples of these restructuring-type joint ventures are: General Electric (United States)-Tungsram, Ganz-Hunsler (United Kingdom) in Hungary; Volkswagen (Germany)-Skoda in the Czech Republic; ABB (Swiss-Swedish)-Zamech, Beloit (United States)-Fampa in Poland.

Generally, the type and scale of management challenges in this category of joint ventures are of a different order than earlier ones and will involve <u>inter alia</u>:

- <u>Liquidity problems</u>. The liquidity of enterprises is strained by: (i) high interest rates (50-100 per cent in some East European countries); (ii) decline in demand at home and from former CMEA markets; (iii) non-payment by customers.

- <u>Threats to home and export markets</u>. The liberalization of imports has meant that enterprise can no longer depend on the formerly captive home markets. The decline in trade with the traditional eastern European customers means that firms must switch their trade to western markets changing in the process the basis of payment to convertible currency in trade with both eastern and western partners.

- <u>Accounting problems</u>. In order to obtain an accurate picture of the performance of the enterprise - both its overall profitability and the performance of each individual production and - the manager will have to introduce new accounting rules for drawing up profit and loss statements and new systems of cost accounting and control.

---

[6] A fuller analysis of these trends is found in <u>Economic Survey of Europe in 1991</u>, Economic Commission for Europe, United Nations, New York, 1991.

- <u>Over-diversified plants</u>. Chronic supply problems forced many enterprises under central planning system to integrate vertically and horizontally. Managers will have to refocus the business operations of these plants on core products and where necessary eliminate other activities. For the same reasons managers will inherit inflated inventories and will have to cut these in order to establish effective cost control.

- <u>Overstaffing</u>. Severe overmanning in many state enterprises in eastern Europe will present joint venture managers with a major human resources problem. If under the conditions of sale for privatization stipulated by the authorities, managers must keep all existing personnel (as in the case of Hungary) then managers will have to explore various alternatives including retraining or consider introducing employment concepts to eastern Europe such as earlier retirement.

- <u>Marketing</u>. The dismantling of the State's distribution network may mean that joint ventures will have to find new outlets for their products. Managers will have to educate local consumers in the value of products and the worth of things like brand-names, after-sales service, maintenance, etc.

- <u>Management of change</u>. Top managers in such enterprises will have to prove themselves adept at managing the multiple stakeholders in the business - employees, government, suppliers, etc. - whilst executing the momentous changes needed to survive. This means educating employees about business realities and the need for change whilst avoiding outright confrontation. It also means encouraging greater performance and rewarding initiative, without provoking envy in a populace not used to gross income disparities.

Managers involved with these problems will be recruited at the senior level, since they will have to possess a broader range and higher level of skills in production, finance and accounting, human resources and marketing. Out of all these, the priority skills for these sorts of ventures appear to be: accounting; restructuring; and marketing.

In the future, it is likely that the earlier types of joint venture operation - small-scale distribution and marketing business - will become bigger as they increase the volume of goods for sale to local markets. Once volumes increase, some enterprises will find it more convenient to produce locally, particularly if their markets are far from their production plants in the West. Managers will then be required to handle both higher volume sales and local production activities.

The second, restructuring-type of joint venture will become more common as privatization and market reforms gather pace in all countries of eastern Europe. Furthermore, joint ventures will be attracted into new industries - e.g. banking and credit activities - and into those sectors where foreign investment has so far been rather small - e.g. the primary sector (oil, mining, etc.). These future investments will require the special training of managers, particularly in banking and financial services where skill requirements are high but where the activity is new for eastern Europe.

Box 3 summarizes the most urgent management training needs confronting management development professionals currently in eastern Europe.

```
┌─────────────────────────────────────────────────────────────────────────┐
│                              BOX 3                                        │
│                                                                           │
│            THE MOST URGENT MANAGEMENT TRAINING NEEDS                       │
│                                                                           │
│         -  General Management (in market economy)                         │
│         -  Strategic Management (planning, portfolio analysis, etc.)       │
│         -  Restructuring (privatization, downsizing, business valuation,   │
│            etc.)                                                           │
│         -  Marketing                                                       │
│         -  Financial Management (sources of funds, equity, capital         │
│            markets, etc.)                                                  │
│         -  Accounting and Auditing                                        │
│         -  Innovation, Technology Management, Product Design               │
│         -  Human Resources Development and Motivation                      │
│         -  Information Management                                          │
│         -  Productivity and Quality Management                             │
│         -  International Business, Globalisation, Networking               │
│         -  Negotiating Skills                                              │
│         -  Business Law                                                    │
│                                                                           │
└─────────────────────────────────────────────────────────────────────────┘
```

3.2 WESTERN RESPONSES

Western companies in eastern Europe have adopted various means to meet their management requirements for East-West Joint Ventures:

The recruitment of expatriate managers. A particularly attractive solution for companies is to recruit from the expatriate networks of Hungarians, Czechs, Poles and Russians living in western Europe and the United States.[7] Such managers possess the twin advantages of familiarity with the values, business customs and language of the eastern European country as well as the experience of working in a market economy. Companies, however, have encountered difficulties finding such candidates and then persuading them to relocate to their home countries. For example to induce expatriates to move to eastern Europe, western Companies are paying compensation and hardship allowances. In one survey more than three-quarters of the 21 large multinational companies questioned were paying employees based in countries such as Poland and the Czech and Slovak Republics, on average one third on top of their base pay.[8] Also some enterprises have noted in some eastern European countries a high degree of local staff resentment to the recruitment of expatriate managers.

In-company training. In those cases where companies recruit their managers locally almost all large enterprises send them back to the headquarters or to other firms within the company organization for training. This training can last for a few weeks up to several months. Some large companies provide even longer training. A leading US firm in the chemical industry recruits young staff from a university in the CIS and sends them to subsidiaries of the firm in the West for a period of three years to learn the skills required. This scheme is notable in two aspects: first, a post

---

[7] "Recruiting the Eastern Euro-Executive" by F. Mueller - Maerki <u>Mergers and Acquisitions</u> Winter 1991.

[8] See <u>Personnel Management</u>, May 1992, p.9.

for trainees is not created artificially within the company - they are recruited to work in a job straightaway. Second, after their training is completed the young manager is at liberty to choose to go back to the CIS to take up a post or to be a manager elsewhere in the company. Initial experience with this scheme seems favourable; difficulties in obtaining authorization from governmental institutions concerned over recruiting direct from the university have been resolved. Lacking the resources of large transnational corporations, smaller companies with joint ventures in eastern or central Europe have tended to rely on on-the-job training. Experiences vary, but in general it has been found that getting formal training in the West (particulary for teaching western accounting principles and practices) is preferable.

Management consultants and recruitment specialists. The use by western companies of recruitment-agencies or so-called "head-hunters" to search for candidates for managerial posts in eastern Europe reflects the rising demand of companies for highly qualified management recruits. In response to early demand for European managers for joint ventures, these western based international agencies tended to confine their search to eastern European managers working in the West. Now head hunters are undertaking their search in local eastern European markets for likely candidates. Recruitment agencies report two major problems in finding suitable candidates, namely the very small number of eastern European managers with knowledge and experience of working in a market economy and the absence of certain professional groups in eastern Europe such as specialists in finance, accounting and marketing [9]. According to recruitment specialists in addition to these problems, eastern European candidates for posts with a high degree of responsibility typically demonstrate a number of shortcomings:

- little or no interest in the job itself, only in the amount of pay the job carries;
- lack of motivation; recruits tend to be under the impression that all that is required to satisfy an employer will be their presence at work;
- tendency for candidates to have second jobs (in Hungary western firms are required to include in their contracts with local staff a clause preventing its employees from holding another job).

In spite of this, recruitment agencies are finding eastern Europe a highly profitable market for their activities due to principally two factors :

- in eastern Europe there is no shortage of applicants, for example 4000 applications were made for one new post with IBM in Prague;
- there is a rapid rise in the wages of eastern European managers (and hence higher commissions for the 'head hunters'). For example in Hungary, less than two years ago a manager earned in the region of 10,000 Austrian schillings (AS) per month; now a manager might expect to earn 35,000 AS.

Western companies have however complained that western firms head hunting in eastern Europe for managers often make disastrous choices reflecting their unfamiliarity with the local job market. Consequently, local head-hunting agencies are being developed in eastern European countries to meet this new demand from the West. [10]

---

[9] Le nouveau Quotidien "Les entreprises occidentales à l'Est en manque de cadres", 30 avril 1992.
[10] ibid

Management training schools. As noted later, firms are using western management schools for training. However, so far there is little evidence of firms using eastern European institutes for the same purpose. In contrast certain schools in eastern Europe are being used by western firms for training non-managerial staff, particularly secretaries. Companies are also showing interest in using management training institutes to offer special tailor-made courses which might train the managers of enterprises who are their principal customers. Even some federations of Industry and Chambers of Commerce have begun to run Training Programmes. A notable example is the scheme employed by The Confederation of British Industry (CBI) together with the British Council. Together they have launched a scheme for the training of managers from central and eastern Europe funded under the British Governments "Know-How Fund". This is a five week intensive course with an emphasis on the learning of practical managerial skills. Four weeks of the course is spent in a UK company, giving eastern managers an understanding of market practices. In some countries companies join forces to organize training courses for eastern European managers.

Conclusion

While these strategies - expatriate recruitment, in-company and on- the-job training, special training programmes - may overcome the difficulties of finding and training managers in the short-term, the long term problem of assuring a supply of appropriately qualified managers from the countries in transition remains. Companies which are obliged to use the services of recruitment agencies to find likely candidates incur high costs for the latter's services. While companies in-house long-term training programmes may develop managers for the senior level this still leaves the problem of finding managers at middle and lower levels. Smaller companies are at a particular disadvantage in attempting to meet their own training requirements which are in themselves much greater. Ultimately, in order to sustain the increase in the number of joint venture registrations in the region, more cost-effective, local solutions must be found, involving principally the host countries' management development institutions.

The following cases of joint ventures in Hungary, Belarus and Russia illustrate the different methods used by western firms to address the problem of management and management training in central and eastern Europe.

CASE-STUDY No.1:

HOW GE APPROACHED THE MANAGEMENT PROBLEM IN TUNGSRAM, HUNGARY

General Electric (GE) of the United States of America discovered that a new training programme was not the only thing it needed to do to solve its management problem when it acquired a controlling interest in Hungary's light bulb manufacturer, Tungsram in November 1989. Aside from this, GE also set out to: improve the flow of information among its Hungarian staff; create the conditions for greater staff participation; provide better incentives; encourage internal staff mobility; and to implement staff reductions.

What GE found at Tungsram

Even before arriving GE was warned by consultants and accountants that Tungsram's biggest problem was overstaffing. In 1989, Tungsram had 18,000 workers. By September 1991 GE had cut the number of workers to 13,000 a decline of 28%. Plans for further cutbacks have been made with the long-term goal being to reduce employment to about 10,000 people.

GE also found that Tungsram had too many managers. Instead of the western average of a ratio of 1:7 between its line workers and managerial staff, Tungsram had a ratio of 1:2.5. In addition, too many managerial levels - 11 in all - existed. Purchase orders, for instance, required 24 signatures when GE arrived.

Another problem found by GE was the lack of motivation and discipline. US managers complained about the lack of private initiative and avoidance of decision-making by Tungsram's managers, in particular, lower level managers were not encouraged to take responsibility. All decisions were made at the top. Unrelenting pessimism by all the workforce managers and workers was also quoted as a discouraging factor. The prospect of promotion for its staff was unappealing because managers did not want to move to different plants. Their reluctance reflected the low level of labour mobility in Hungary which despite the country's small-size, lacks the infrastructure for moving staff, e.g. housing estate agents, removal companies, etc.

GE's reorganization steps

GE's first step was to look for a Chief Executive Officer with the right combination of skill for Tungsram. They chose George Varga, an Hungarian who had fled Hungary as a 20 year old in 1956 and had spent 28 years with GE in countries as diverse as Spain, Mexico, Switzerland and the Netherlands. He was in charge of a GE plastics factory in the Netherlands when chosen for Tungsram.

Management reorganization and training

In a total break with the past system GE began encouraging Tungsram's lower-level managers to take responsibility for their own decisions. Under the previous system, managers at various levels in the organization did not pay a lot of attention to the management of people, motivating and leading them. Decisions tended to come as commands from the top, so that management at various levels was reduced simply to following decisions already taken from above. GE wanted a freer, more informal environment in which department managers could take decisions and have more authority to manage the people under them.

To do this managers had to be trained. GE introduced three programmes from its own university in Coronville, U.S.A. One was for factory foremen and supervisors, another for junior-level management - those with one-five years experience - and the third for the more experienced manager. By the beginning of 1992, 380 people had been put through those programmes.

GE was aware that its own general programmes might have to be adapted to suit the peculiar needs of a management brought up under a central planned system. Thus, before introducing these programmes they sent their English-speaking Hungarians to the United States of America to examine the programmes and decide whether they were suitable for the Hungarian culture and environment. When the response of its Hungarian staff was positive the programmes were translated into Hungarian and slightly modified to suit Tungsram's particular needs.

The basic course for foremen and supervisors teaches fundamental management skills, management of a team and how to appraise individual performance. The next level for junior managers teaches how to motivate employees, to encourage them, how to consider salary increases and similar matters.

In order to break the previous system where commands were passed from the top, GE now forces its managers and supervisors to sit down with their team of workers and produce a rationale and logic for what they are doing.

Communicating with its workforce

One of GE's first decisions was to improve the flow of information to Tungsram managers and employees about what was happening in their company. GE found that the typical communications channels of a western company did not exist in Tungsram. Managers in a western company would have channelled information to their workforce but at Tungsram the management had no experience of doing this.

Thus, GE created a communications department to organize large-scale meetings of employees and management, developed an internal radio system and widened the scope of the company newsletter: Tungsram now publishes a General Company Newsletter with 10 local issues for the various plants around the country. The company also hired a Hungarian-born consultant with many years experience in in-house communications in North America. As a result, there are now trained communications officers in each of Tungsram's plants. They inform staff about the changes which are taking place; why the number of employees are being reduced; why it is important to make the product cost-efficient, etc.

Encouraging people to take responsibility

GE is also encouraging more decision-making at lower levels with a new concept it calls "work out". A group of employees are brought together to discuss a particular business challenge and to see if it can be made more simply and efficiently. Discussions are guided at present by senior management but GE's aim is to reduce top management involvement so that eventually the workforce feels able to take the responsibility themselves.

Wages

GE found that the previous management of Tungsram had maintained a bewildering system of variable bonuses. There were different systems in various departments and even within departments. Some of the bonuses depended on circumstances beyond the control of the individual worker. For instance if necessary material did not arrive on schedule the production line could not meet its target. The cause of the problem could lie elsewhere in the company or even outside it. GE decided to eliminate most of the bonuses and merge them with the base pay. By the end of 1990 both operators and white collar-workers were receiving a more predictable rate of pay.

One of GE's innovations at Tungsram was to introduce the concept of differentiated pay based on performance and a system of performance appraisal in which two managers have to assess an individual's work. Again Tungsram brought in training programme to teach managers how performance should be assessed. So far, 780 managers and supervisors have completed the training course.

To implement staff reduction of 4,700 in its first year of operations, GE management introduced a programme of early retirement, a freeze on new recruitment and a restructuring which resulted in some people leaving voluntarily. 400, however, were made redundant.

Assessment

The problem GE found and its method of dealing with it will not be dissimilar from the experience of other companies venturing into eastern Europe. However, Tungsram itself, a multinational company manufacturing high quality products for western markets and GE, the world's fifth largest company in 1991, are far from the typical eastern or western enterprise. The central problem for GE was the authoritarian structure of management authority in Tungsram which required reorganization in order to give managers more power and confidence to take decisions. This was however essentially a solution for middle and lower management. To solve the problem at the top GE brought with it to Tungsram its own 10 man management team. Its hope is that Hungarians will eventually take over senior management positions when they gain more experience. It is too early to a judge how successful GE's reorganization has been: however after two years under new management, the Company is still losing money. In 1992, the company made a HUF 9 bn (USD 104 mn) loss, the biggest in Hungarian corporate history.

CASE-STUDY No.2:

THE MANAGEMENT CHALLENGE IN BELARUS: THE CASE OF AGV-POLOTSK [11]

The small Italian firm AGV began in 1946 by manufacturing saddles for bicycles, and in 1947, became the world's first motorcycle helmet producer. Today, Italian companies are the main exporters of helmets around the world, with AGV as their leader. In Italy, the company produces about 600,000 helmets annually, 70% of which are for export, making AGV the second largest motorcycle helmet exporter worldwide. In total, AGV exports to over 30 countries, including those of Europe, the United States, Japan, Canada, and Australia, and has over 1,500 sales outlets worldwide. The firm employs about 190 people in the industrial district of Spinetta Marengo near the town of Alessandria in northern Italy and its annual sales reached USD 60 million in 1991.

This factory produces helmets in fibreglass and kevlar. Although from production methods cannot be categorized as "high tech", they are nevertheless technologically advanced with the moulding, cutting and varnishing stages carried out using automation. Instead of employing in-house engineers, the company consults with an outside research centre which studies the design and graphics of helmets to be developed and manufactured. AGV also runs a laboratory which is fully equipped to carry out safety tests on its helmets, which allows for certification of the helmets according to regulations in Europe, the United States, Japan, Australia and Canada.

---

[11] Another version of this case-study appears in "Small and Medium-Sized Enterprises in the ECE Region", UN/ECE (forthcoming).

Traditionally, the motorcycle helmet manufacturing industry has been characterized by high costs and a downward trend in demand. The high cost of production results mainly from the cost of importing the fibreglass to produce the helmets, and saturated markets tend to reduce further demand for the product. Although costs remain high, the recent switch of motorcycle helmets from a "necessity" to a "fashion accessory" has brought the industry renewed growth, especially in the United States.

Description of the joint venture

*In 1990, AGV became a partner in the joint venture AGV-Polotsk in Polotsk, Belarus, about 200 kilometres outside of Minsk. The joint venture's other partner is Steklovolokno, a fibreglass manufacturer and **formerly a military defence firm**, which is located in Polotsk. The aim of the joint venture is twofold: to produce and supply motorcycle helmets to all of the republics of the ex-Soviet Union and to other countries of former CMEA; and to re-export unfinished fibreglass helmet shells to AGV in Italy for final production and sale in the West. The current level of production at AGV-Polotsk is 160,000 helmets annually, compared to the 600,000 produced annually by AGV in Italy. The joint venture is labour-intensive and currently employs 80 workers. AGV holds a 40% share in AGV-Polotsk while Steklovolokno holds 60%. The company has a representative office in Minsk in order to facilitate marketing and sales efforts.*

Strategies of the partners

There were several reasons to explain AGV's decision to establish a joint venture in Belarus. The first most important consideration was the fact that its selected local partner could provide its main raw material (fibreglass) more cheaply than from its traditional source in France. Another was low labour costs. Rather than producing the fibreglass helmet shells in Italy, AGV is exporting to Italy a portion of the shells produced in Polotsk for final processing, which will save AGV approximately 70% on its cost of production in Italy. This strategy will be particularly useful for exporting to the USA, as the firm presently finds selling to the U.S. market very expensive because of the high insurance costs there (approximately 80% of the product's regular cost). In other world markets, the insurance costs represents only on average 1% of the product's cost. Thus, the helmets completed by AGV in Italy from shells produced in Belarus will overcome some of the cost barriers in selling to the US market.

Other aspects of AGV's strategy include potential gains from operating in the vast market of the former Soviet Union. The company estimates that in this market of 300 million inhabitants, there are approximately 30 million cyclists who are required by law to wear helmets. Despite this requirement, motorcycle helmets were not manufactured in the region until AGV-Polotsk began operations. Individual republics are planning to introduce regulations on helmets quality which will be common to the entire region, and there also are plans for a sole testing laboratory covering all the republics. A director has been chosen for the laboratory; but the latter still has to be set up. For the moment, the only laboratory in operation is in AGV-Polotsk. Consequently, AGV-Polotsk is well ahead of any new competitors on these markets.

Often, the strategy of eastern partners in a joint venture is to acquire managerial and technological upgrading in addition to foreign capital. However, the aim of Steklovolokno is essentially to convert from military activities to civilian firm. As well, the company is currently being privatized and therefore must achieve financial independence. At the moment, AGV is loaning money to Steklovolokno to ensure its participation because the firm has no currency to buy spare parts, equipment, etc. If the joint venture goes bankrupt, AGV has the option to buy its stock of fibreglass or take over the company. However, the joint venture would not benefit if one of its partners fails.

Locating a partner

The founding of AGV-Polotsk was helped by the fact that AGV's management had had business contacts in the former Soviet Union for some years. In 1988, one of the firm's directors had a casual meeting with the president of the Moscow's Chamber of Commerce to whom he presented several AGV's products. Soon after, AGV was invited to show its products at a meeting of representatives of the Chamber of Commerce in several republics. This presentation was soon followed by various business proposals to AGV. Since, AGV kept in contact with the fibreglass manufacturer Steklovolokno, it arranged to have the factory moved to Polotsk, Belarus.

The original contract to form the joint venture was signed in Moscow in 1989, because at that time, the fibreglass company was under the jurisdiction of the Central Chemical Ministry for the Soviet Union. AGV was responsible for providing the government with a feasibility study on the economic prospects of the joint venture over the next 10 years in both foreign and local currency terms. However, when Belarus claimed its independence, the contract had to be re-signed under the new government of Belarus in 1990.

Financing

Although AGV-Polotsk received a 3-year tax holiday, political uncertainties made financial guarantees difficult to obtain. Under the original agreement signed in 1989, the central government in Moscow was the financial backer. The government of Belarus is now the official guarantor, although these guarantees are in roubles. In essence, the real backer to the joint venture was the Italian government, as the debt of the joint venture is owed to the Italian bank, Medio Credito. The initial capital to create the joint venture was 1.5 million roubles. Originally, AGV took a 40% share in the venture and Steklovolokno 60% in order to expedite the registration process. This meant, that under the old exchange rate, AGV contributed USD 1 million in cash and the eastern partner USD 1.5 million to the joint venture.

Aside from the start-up capital, the investment in equipment and technology for the venture was supplied by AGV in Italy, and paid for by a USD 10 million loan to the joint venture by Medio Credito. The joint venture paid the bank by its exports of unfinished goods (helmet shells) to AGV in Italy for hard currency; AGV then refunded Medio Credito. In this way, AGV (Italy) took no risk. The Italian government was in effect the main risk taker.

Management

One of the greatest obstacles faced by AGV-Polotsk was the management of its newly established joint venture. It became obvious to the Italian side that the running of the plant could not be left to local managers using their old practices. Local management knew nothing about marketing. They had never needed to sell their products, to inform prospective customers about their products or to find out about the competition to their activities. In production, concepts of time and depreciation did not exist. However, as a minority shareholder in the venture, AGV had no power to choose the managers or to fill the top post. The company was thus initially run by a manager from Belarus. In an effort to improve the quality of the local management AGV paid for 30 managers to come to Italy to train alongside their counterparts in their Italian factory and to obtain the skills they would perform back in Belarus. Thus an Italian administration manager taught his job to his Belorussian counterpart; an Italian production manager showed his counterpart his job in Italy and so on. In each case a translator was required to assist in the teaching. This proved enormously expensive to AGV and was ultimately unsuccessful. The Belorussian managers were not able to learn what they should do at home and were reluctant to give up a life-time of experience.

Thus AGV resolved that it had to obtain majority control of the venture in order to be able to put its own managers into the important company positions and thus bought a further 20 % stake in the joint venture. The company believed that had it not done this, poor local management would have quickly led to the joint venture's total failure. An Italian was thus put in overall charge. Purchasing and Marketing Departments were set up. Italian managers were appointed to posts in sales and production. Local procurement remained however the responsibility of the local manager.

However, the arrival of Italians to be managers in these key areas created further problems. It was difficult to find Italians who knew Belorussian or Russian and could do this work. It was also not easy for Italian managers to be accepted as part of the local management team. Although the scope for using local senior management remain limited, AGV has been very satisfied with younger employees in middle management positions. The firm noted their high literacy levels, the high quality of their technical training and their strong support of market reforms. The firm is planning to train its young employees according to western methods and to reward work well done. AGV is confident that young managers will, in a few years, operate the company without western assistance.

Assessment

Concerning the management problem encountered by AGV in Belarus a number of lessons can be learned: First, even finding one of the region's most efficient enterprises did not obviate the need to recruit more suitable managers to run the enterprise. Second, in setting up a joint venture, western partners should try to acquire a majority share in order to assume overall management control. Thirdly, it may not be worthwhile to train senior managers; where resources are limited, training should be focused instead on younger management personnel.

CASE-STUDY No.3:

PUTTING THE LOCALS IN CHARGE: THE CASE OF THE RUSSIAN-AMERICAN JOINT VENTURE, DIALOGUE[12]

Dialogue

"Without much question, the most successful American-Russian joint venture that has been established is a company called Dialogue.

At about the time Gorbachev came to power in 1986, a Chicagoan named Joe Ritchie began taking an active interest in the Soviet Union. A founder of a highly successful options trading company in Chicago, Ritchie had no specific business experience in the USSR, but he clearly grasped the country's enormous latent potential. On a visit to Moscow, he had a chance meeting with a Russian computer scientist named Pyotr Zrelov, designer and manager of the management

---

[12] This Case-study is taken from an article "Joint Ventures in Russia: Put the Locals in Charge" written by Paul R. Lawrence and Charalambos A. Vlatchoutsicos, Harvard Business School Press, January-February 1993.

information systems at Kamaz, one of Russia's largest truck manufacturers. The two men liked each other from the start and spent several days getting to know one another. They discovered that they agreed about how the world worked and how it might work better. Within a matter of months, they had put together the rudiments of a business deal. Their goal was to create nothing less than the Russian equivalent of IBM - a full-fledged, integrated computer company for the world's largest nation. In late 1987, Dialogue came into being with the signing of a joint-venture agreement, only the second with a partner based in the United States.

To form the venture, Zrelov and Ritchie picked strong, specialised partners. Kamaz, Moscow State University, the Central Institute of Economics and Applied Mathematics, the Space Research Institute, and the Soviet Experimental Computer Centre at the National Exhibition of Economic Achievements were all original participants in the joint venture.

Ritchie put up USD 5 million for a 22% share of the company, while the Soviets put up SUR 15 million for the remainder. From the very beginning of Dialogue's operations, Ritchie stepped into the background, making it clear to employees, vendors, and government officials that he had fully empowered Zrelov to run the show.

Five years later, through offices in 34 cities, Dialogue has sold and serviced more than half of the personal computers installed in the former Soviet Union. Dialogue sells its Russian software all over the world and maintains ten offices in Europe, Japan, and the United States. It employs 3,500 people throughout the states that were once the Soviet Union and 700 elsewhere. Capitalized as a joint stock company, Dialogue motivates its managers by allowing them to purchase stock at advantageous prices and so share in the profits of the company they are helping to create.

Pyotr Zrelov, with wide authority over company operations, has been key to the venture's success. He has mastered the basic business of his company, he has faced down high-handed government authorities, he has recruited and trained managers to set up new offices, and time and again he has plunged the company into new businesses when these seemed the best solution to some stubborn problem. Hindered by the general lack of basic goods and services, Dialogue has started a bank, a construction company, an architectural firm, an auditing service, dental clinics, a law firm, a securities brokerage, and a stock exchange, to name only a few. Frustrated by the notoriously backward Russian phone system, Dialogue is now in the process of installing its won telecommunications network, establishing 200 local exchanges, and linking them together.

This may seem startlingly bold to a western observer, but it smacks of the self-sufficiency factories had to demonstrate in the old Soviet Union to cope with constant shortages. Lacking horizontal market structures, a Russian tractor factory, for instance, might make not only batteries, drive shafts, axles, engines, wheels, and other components, but also refrigerators and other hard-to-find consumer products either for its employees or to barter for supplies. Each collective enterprise was a self-contained fiefdom of interlocking interests.

Ritchie does not disagree with the common observation that most Russians are not natural entrepreneurs. He argues, however, that most Americans are not either. He believes that the percentage of entrepreneurs in each population is about the same. He then points out compellingly that Dialogue has made well over USD 100 million net on an initial investment of USD 5 million by leaving all salient operating decisions to Russian managers who, in the conventional view, lacked both entrepreneurial instincts and capitalistic training.

Ritchie credits Zrelov for his skills as a leader and decision maker. Zrelov, in turn, gives much of the credit to enlightened owners who allow him the freedom to act. Both men advise companies considering joint ventures to search not just for a general manager and partner, but also for a friend. A strong leader with intelligence, connections, high integrity, and a sense of adventure may not be easy to find, but the business opportunities surely outweigh the frustrations and hard work of a patient search and a long-term commitment."

Conclusion

This case-study acts as a counter balance to the conventional wisdom that if joint ventures are to be successful, local management should be either replaced by western ones or be subject to tight controls and require advance approval for all significant decisions. It demonstrates that if western companies wish to be successful in Russia's unique business environment, they require managers with local knowledge and empowered with real decision-taking authority.

4. MANAGEMENT DEVELOPMENT AND TRAINING PRACTICES

4.1 MANAGEMENT TRAINING IN THE EAST BEFORE AND AFTER

In determining from where and how new management skills might be generated in the East, it would be an error to disregard completely the traditional management training institutes which had performed under central planning. For a start it should not be overlooked that under central planning, management training took place extensively at various levels:

Top level - in a Central Management School (or in the regional affiliates of the School) for senior ministry officials, directors of large business organizations (employing at least 20,000 employees), bank directors, top scientists, engineers and government officials;

Second level - at the Ministerial or sectoral level for directors and managers of small and medium-size enterprises and department heads of large business organizations;

Third level - within state enterprises themselves. For example, the Zil automotive plant, which produces the "Russian cadillacs" and was renowned for producing the best trucks in the former USSR had its own management school complete with its own dean, established curricula and teaching materials.

Governing these educational establishments were elaborate systems of rules. For example: all managers at all levels had to be educated in management; no manager could be promoted without first being educated for the higher position; and all managers had to be "retrained" every three to five years (In Poland, some retraining was required annually). A substantial infrastructure of teaching facilities, lecture theatres, equipment and staff for management was thus created.

The essential difference between these schools and western establishments was that in the East management was not taught as a profession. The manager in eastern Europe grew up as a scientist or an engineer not as a professional manager who could go from industry to industry as in the West. Students graduating from one of the above-mentioned second-level training establishments and presenting a dissertation would qualify for a doctoral degree not in management but in each participant's field of specialization. From a western perspective, schools taught something similar to public administration. The principal subjects were "scientific management" and "scientific work organization" that is work studies, time and motion studies, and other elements of industrial engineering.

Nonetheless, eastern training establishments were in the process of modernizing themselves when the communist system collapsed. A whole new spectrum of subjects began to be introduced in the mid and late 1980s which began to concentrate on the organization of work and methods of improving efficiency: automating processes, installing computers, quality control. It should also be remembered that a few schools even at this time had developed close links with western counterparts. For example, top managers from the former USSR - Fiat automobile plant attended classes as result of collaboration between the Academy of National Economy and Sogea University in Genoa.

Thus, in making management training in the East more appropriate to the emerging market economy, it is not necessary for eastern European administrators and their western consultants to start from scratch. Equally, implanting everything from the West rather than building on what they have, would be a serious mistake.

However, the present problems of managers in the countries of eastern Europe and the rapid change of conditions created by the slow process of economic reform has led many of these countries to develop a highly technique-oriented and superficial "quick fix" approach towards learning western managerial methods. This approach, along with the lack of a meaningful professional code of values renders high quality management education in eastern Europe all the more necessary. A recent study indicates that the diversity of the central and East European Institutions presently collaborating with US universities and colleges reflects a growing decentralization of academic authority, both at the national and institutional levels.[13] It also indicates a great variance in the quality between the various training programmes offered by local and foreign private and governmental institutions.

Seeking a higher quality of management education to reform or create new curricula in various fields and seeking long-denied opportunities for scholarly contact with western specialists, universities have vigorously developed new links with various western partners. However, many western Universities have indicated some frustration at the lack of co-ordination within institutions and the fact that new administrators have little experience with foreign exchanges. Their eastern European counterparts frequently express similar frustration in reverse at the lack of US co-ordination and understanding of the conditions in eastern Europe.

Nonetheless, the creation of new institutions to serve both qualitatively and quantitatively the new requirements for management personnel is occurring rapidly as a result of two trends: on the one hand, previous founded institutions are adapting their courses and programmes to fit the new requirements while, on the other, totally new establishments are being founded. A good example of the first trend are many Universities faculties of economics - at which level students were never previously taught management - moving into the field of business administration and marketing and indeed preparing to offer MBA style programmes. For the other trend, there are now established in many central and eastern Europe a variety of different institutions - most in the private or semi-private sector - offering a broad spectrum of courses designed to prepare managers for market economies.

There follows a brief description in each of the economies in transition on the progress in establishing new management training institutes.

---

[13] "Where Walls once stood, US Responses to New Opportunities of Academic Co-operation with Eastern-Central Europe", Mary E. Kirk, 2nd Report of the East Central Europe Information Exchange Institute of International Education, 1992.

Bulgaria

Bulgaria has five principal management development centres:

- Sofia International Management School
- Institute of Management and Administration
- Business School at the Ministry of Foreign Trade
- Department of Management, Higher Institute of Economics
- Centre for Organization and Management, Bulgaria Industrial Associations.

Western management schools played some part in the development of Bulgarian business education. Now these traditional schools are being restructured, with the help of western training establishments. For example in Sofia, the United Kingdom's Cranfield School of Management is advising the authorities on the redevelopment of teaching programmes in the Sophia International Management School.

Commonwealth of Independent States

Although developments in Management Training are taking place primarily within individual republics, pan Commonwealth organizations promoting the teaching of management do exist.

In 1990 the Association of Schools of International Business was founded comprising 29 member schools from the CIS, to render assistance in developing business schools in the CIS. The Association undertakes many activities. It brings together CIS business schools with foreign business schools; cooperates with the European Foundation for Management Development (EFMD) and the American Assembly of Collegiate Schools of Business (AACSB); creates international funds for financing the promotion of CIS business schools; attempts to raise the proficiency of the teaching staff and to improve teaching methods; seeks to promote the process of accreditation of the emerging CIS business schools and management centres; and provides a directory of members and non-member Schools throughout the CIS.

Russian Federation

Reflecting the progress made by management schools in adapting to the new economic reality, in 1992 two western multinational companies - Siemens and Xerox - hired several graduates from local business schools for their joint ventures in Moscow. Such progress is remarkable given the fact that a little earlier schools in management were relatively few and virtually exclusively designed to train managers for the Centrally Planned Economic System. Each Ministry had its own institute to train managers in the industry for which it was responsible. These institutes were mainly located in Moscow. Only 30 affiliates of these institutes were located in the rest of the Soviet Union. Aside from these Moscow-based Ministries, 7 republican Governments had founded management training institutes in their own territories funded out of their own budgets. No other institute nor person was permitted to train managers. Nobody paid for the education received under this system; everything was paid for out of state budgets.

In 1989 this system collapsed. The enterprises themselves began to pay for the training of their managers, all restrictions on "business" schools were lifted and new "management" institutes mushroomed.

This new found freedom however brought with it a number of difficulties. The new schools operating under no centrally or academically approved accreditation system were free to award students "certificates of management" for payment rather than for any knowledge attained. So-called "management courses" run at Black Sea Coast resorts represented a form of academic tourism which had little to do with education. Moreover, with the collapse of the industrial Ministries, the principal source of funding for the traditional management training institutes dried up. Consequently several stopped their training of managers. Others changed. The Institute for Tourism for example, became the school of International Business and Tourism.

In spite of these difficulties a few top quality schools have emerged (see Box 4) in Russia with a well trained faculty, close links with western management institutes (see Box 5) and good relations with local, and in a few cases, foreign businesses. The creation of such schools was not only due to the need for training in the new emerging economic system. With the fall in the value of the rouble, it became prohibitively expensive to send Russian managers for training in the West. A large percentage of these top schools' teachers have been trained in the West and many now offer standard MBA programmes. Where the schools lack expertise is in, for example, accounting or corporate finance; in these cases, representatives from western based accounting firms are often hired to teach courses on these subject.

In the short time these top schools have been operating, a number of changes have also taken place in the student profile. First, students who take courses now predominantly come from the private or semi-private sector rather than from the state sector as in the recent past. In 1991, for example, 30 % of students undertaking the one year programme at the Academy of the National Economy belonged to the non-state sector. In 1992, the figure had risen to 72 % per cent. Students too are getting younger. In 1991 in the same school almost 60 % of students were over 35. In 1992, 82 % were under 35.

BOX 4

THE TOP 15 BUSINESS SCHOOLS IN THE RUSSIAN FEDERATION

In a supplement of the Russian newspaper Izvestia, is produced weekly in partnership with the Financial Times, there has been recently published the results of a survey of businessmen to discover the top business schools operating in Russia at present. Respondents made their selection from a total of 120 of the biggest business schools, taking into account the following criteria:

- the scope of the school's programme and the extent to which it covers the full range of subjects dealing with business education, banking, auditing, etc.;
- the content of the programme;
- the availability and length of programmes dealing with, marketing and management;
- quality of teaching staff and the use of external specialist teachers with business experience.

BOX 4 (Continued)

The top 15 chosen were ranked as follows:

1. International Business School MGIMO of the Moscow State Institute for International Relations (MGIMO) (76 prospekt Vernadskogo, 117 454 Moscow);

2. High School of International Business of the Academy of National Economy under the Government of the Russian Federation (82 prospekt Vernadskogo, 117 571 Moscow);

3. St.-Petersburg Institute of International Management (IMISP)
(P.O. Box 450, "IMISP", 199 034 St.-Petersburg);

4. High Commercial School of the Ministry of Foreign Economic Relations of the Russian Federation (32 Levoberejnaya ul., 125 475 Moscow);

5. International Moscow Finance and Banking School (1 Kibalchich ul., 129 848 Moscow);

6. International Management School "Lati-Lovanium" (5 Prof. Popov ul., 197 376 St.-Petersburg);

7. Centre of Management Training under the Moscow Institute of the National Economy named after Plehanov (41 Zatsepa ul., 113 054 Moscow);

8. Moscow International Business School (MIRBIS) (28 Stremianni per, 113 054 Moscow);

9. Russian Academy of management (84 prospekt Vernadskogo, 117 571 Moscow);

10. Management Centre under the State Academy of Management named after Ordjonikidze (99 Riazanski prospekt, 109 542 Moscow);

11. Kaliningrad School of International Business (17 Kirov ul., 236 000 Kaliningrad);

12. Nizhniy Novgorod Institute of International Business (31A Minina ul., 603 155 Nizhniy);

13. Voroneg High School of Entrepreneurs (50, Nikitinskya ul., 394 000 Voroneg);

14. Moscow International School "Business in Industry and Science" (MISBIS)
(9 Miousskya pl., bureau 261, 125 190 Moscow);

15. International Centre of High Business Administration under the Diplomatic Academy (53/2 Ostogenka ul., 119 021 Moscow).

Source: Izvestia/Finansovic Izvestia, 10-16 December 1992.

BOX 5

EUROPEAN BUSINESS SCHOOLS, ACTIVE ON THE RUSSIAN MARKET

Assisted with grants from the EC Tempus Programme or out of their own resources, many European business schools have established links with counterpart Institutions in Russia. The following European educational establishments are in some capacity now present in Russia.

GERMANY

Carl Duisberg Gesellschaft
Personal und Management Beratung GmbH
Deutsche Management Akademie Niedersachsen GmbH
Ministry of Economy and Technology of Hessen
AE "Deutsche Bank"
DBB Akademie
Frauenhofer Institut für Materialfluß und Logistik
Institut für Unternehmensführung

SWITZERLAND

Hochschule St. Gallen für Wirtschafts-, Rechts
und Sozialwissenschaften

ITALY

ENFAPI - SOGEA
NOMISMA (Societa di Studi Economici S.p.A)
ISVOR - FIAT S.p.A (Societa di Sviluppo e
    Addestamento Industriale)
UNIONQUADRI

SWEDEN

BITS (Swedish Agency for International Technical
and Economic Cooperation)

UNITED KINGDOM

London Business School
Coventry University (Mr. R. Wesley)
Warwick Business School
Manchester Polytechnic (Business School)
Kingston Polytechnic
Henley School of Business

```
┌─────────────────────────────────────────────────────────────┐
│                                                             │
│                     BOX 5 (Continued)                       │
│                                                             │
│                         FRANCE                              │
│                                                             │
│             ACTIM                                           │
│             Ecole Nationale d'Aministration (ENA)           │
│             ESSEC                                           │
│             INSEAD                                          │
│             Institut supérieur de Gestion                   │
│             Chambre de Commerce et d'Industrie de Paris     │
│             SEFRI                                           │
│             Centre de Perfectionnement aux Affaires         │
│                                                             │
│                         FINLAND                             │
│                                                             │
│             Institute of Technology, Helsinki               │
│                                                             │
│                         BELGIUM                             │
│                                                             │
│             University of Louvanium                         │
│             Arthur K. Watson International Education Centre, La Hulpe │
│                                                             │
└─────────────────────────────────────────────────────────────┘
```

Ukraine

In the former Soviet Union, during the period of <u>Perestroika</u>, several management schools were established in conjunction with support from western management institutions. The first manifestation of this new found East-West cooperation in the management field was in Kiev, Ukraine. Here under the inspiration of the Canadian-Ukrainian director of the International Management Institute (IMI) in Geneva , Mr. Bohdan Hawrylyschyn, the IMI Kiev was established. The international orientation of this new school is immediately evident in the choice of languages in which instruction takes place: English, German, Russian and Ukrainian. Care was taken that the beneficiaries of IMI's Kiev's course - leading officials of Ministries, Chief Executive Officers of companies and academies - should not be taught in pure management theory but through study trips abroad and in workshop with leading foreign management specialists, should obtain the necessary practical experience as well. The IMI Kiev in addition is not only active in the teaching of managers, but also, through research and publication actively promotes the transition to a market economy in the Ukraine.

Former Czech and Slovak Federal Republic

The Czech and Slovak Federal Republic in the past was known as one of the most orthodox eastern European countries. Since the "velvet revolution" there has been a great demand for western-style management training. Through collaboration with local management schools, German Institutes of Management are particulary engaged in the training of Czech and Slovak managers.

In February 1990, for instance, the European Business School from Oestrich-Winkel (EBS) founded in cooperation with a Federation of Manufacturers of machine tools and Management Institutes the Czech and Slovak Federal Republic, an affiliate school in Prague. In their programme the eastern Manager must take courses in English and German and spend a two months' practical work in a German company. The EBS-Prague differs form its western European counterpart in an a number of ways. Rather than teaching undergraduates, the programmes are devised for practising managers.

In 1992 an OECD study into University Education in the former Czech and Slovak Federal Republic noted the diversity of study programmes and degrees and the absence of specialized management studies leading to an MBA type degree. Currently the country has several American business schools offering MBA programmes and these fill a niche in the market for business education; but it is a small niche and it is very expensive. It is felt that a far larger number of managers and other students would attend a local business school where the instruction was bilingual (English and Czech) and the programme was not a distinctively American programme, but one which adapts market education to the culture, experience and history of the local Czech people.

To this end the University of Economics, Prague, has created the Prague International Business School (PIBS) to offer business students training and degree study comparable with those in Europe and the USA. It is hoped that graduates will be able to apply for jobs with international institutions and companies either at home or abroad. The PIBS, in its attempt to emulate the world's leading business schools, offers:

- an international faculty;
- bilingual training, first language English;
- a basic core curriculum consisting of Accounting and Finance, Quantitative Analysis, Business Policy, Marketing, Human Resources Management, Organizational Behaviour and Economics;
- own case studies;
- an emphasis on practical training.

Hungary

The leading country in the former eastern European bloc in the provision of management education is Hungary where efforts to improve management using western market models have been going on for many years. Accordingly, Hungary is now home to some of the region's leading management training schools. For example, the International Management Centre in Budapest can claim the title of being the first private Business School in eastern Europe. Thanks to its link with the University of Pittsburgh in the USA, students of the IMC can enrol in the American University's MBA programme.

In addition, the country's four major universities, Budapest University of Economic Sciences (BUES), Technical University of Budapest, Janus Pannonius University in Pecs, and Miskolc University, are revising their training programmes to cater for market-oriented management. Hungary has also a strong tradition of specialised colleges, for instance the colleges of Tourism and Catering, and of Finance and Accountancy.

Poland

Poland has a relatively long tradition of western style management education starting in the late XIX century. This tradition has never been completely discontinued. In the 70s and 80s Polish management education systems were considerably upgraded by American and German foundations (mainly Ford, Fulbright, Kosciuszko and Humboldt foundations) offering scholarships to Polish educators and researchers.

Diversity is one of the main features of the Polish management education system. The current structure includes at least four major types of public and non-public training institutions:

- School of Management of Warsaw University and management departments at several universities (including universities of economics);
- Newly created non-public business schools (40-80 nationwide);
- Profit-oriented training companies and training centres (some 80-100 nationwide);
- Hundreds of consulting firms occasionally involved in training.

The oldest and the biggest is the Warsaw University School of Management established in 1972 with current enrolment of 1500. The school is now offering 5 different kinds of programmes:

- Master programme, lasting 5 years for full time students;
- Master programme, lasting 5 years for part-time students (weekend classes);
- Bachelor programme, lasting 3 years for part-time students (evening classes);
- Master programme, lasting 2 years for post-graduate students (weekend classes);
- Post-graduate executive programme, lasting 1 year for part-time students (weekend classes).

Alongside the School of Management at Warsaw University operates the International Postgraduate Management Centre. The Centre confers upon its alumnus a joint Warsaw University and the University of Illinois (Urbana Champaigne) MBA degree.

Since 1992 the situation of the public schools vis-à-vis non-public schools is rapidly changing because according to the newly passed law they are allowed to charge fees for the education of students with the exception of full time students.

Romania

The origin of management training in Romania can be traced to the 1940s when management disciplines were introduced into school and college curricula. In the 1960s both the UNDP and ILO advised the Government on the founding of the new CEPECA Management Development Centre. Its objectives included:

- training managerial personnel: improving their management skills and increasing their knowledge using methods borrowed from the industrially developed countries.

- conducting research with a view to adapting to domestic environments management techniques applied elsewhere in the world.

4.2 WESTERN CONTRIBUTION TO MANAGEMENT DEVELOPMENT

The European Community (particularly the TEMPUS programme) and individual western European countries (e.g., the U.K.'s Know-How Fund) rapidly implemented a wide variety of programmes supporting cooperation and greater mobility for eastern European students and scholars. As noted in the previous section , western firms are using management schools in the West to send their managers for training. Some western business schools, either independently or in collaboration with eastern counterparts, are already actively engaged in the training of managers from these countries. Such activities include:

- provision of courses and programmes for eastern European managers in the West;
- setting up of MBA courses in the countries in transition;
- organization of teacher and student exchanges with management schools and institutions in eastern Europe;
- establishment of programmes to train trainers from eastern European management schools.

A study undertaken by the Institute of International Education of the USA provides an overview of the activities of western management schools in the countries of eastern Europe. Although this study covers only US Universities, it can be assumed that its findings are largely true for western management schools as a whole. These findings pointed to:

- A substantial growth in both the number of exchange programmes and the US institutions sponsoring them. 176 US Institutions reported on some 330 collaborative projects with eastern European partners. This represents a threefold increase in the number of programmes and exchange agreements listed in a similar study carried out in 1990.

- A decline in the predominance of long-term broad rang reciprocal exchange agreements. The study finds that the majority of programmes at present are limited in duration and fields of study, by design, providing short-term, high impact training.

- An increasing number of academic and professional training programmes at present are taking place on-site in central and eastern Europe, reflecting in part the emphasis funding agencies placed on targeted programme areas and lower in-country training costs.

- A high number of exchange and training programmes in professional fields, including management, most of which have been initiated since 1990.

- A predominance of programme activity in the northern and central regions (Poland, Czech and Slovak Federal Republic, and Hungary), with Bulgaria, Romania, CIS, Baltic Republics and countries of the former Yugoslavia lagging well behind.

- Joint research projects and study abroad programmes for US students display a broader geographic range than was possible two years ago.

- Professional and technical training programmes comprise the largest group of initiatives administered by US universities in the countries of eastern Europe (46 out of 333 programmes). A majority of these projects are intended to promote entrepreneurial activities, execute training, or other skills required for the successful transition to market-driven economies. While some Conferences, workshops, and other short-term activities are the primary vehicles for such training, many of the programmes focus on the development of cadres in professional sectors within certain countries or across the region.

(1)   Short-term courses in western business schools

So far, the most common of these initiatives and the one which has the most direct impact on the training of managers for East-West joint ventures are the special courses for eastern managers which are held in management schools in the West. Lasting from periods ranging from two weeks to three months, these courses typically comprise classroom teaching and study visits to local enterprises. Sometimes the student undertakes in-house training with a local firm. Often the trainee is the eastern European manager of a joint venture who is being sponsored by his western business partner. Typical of many such courses is the one run by the Fuqua School of Business of Duke University, North Carolina, United States, details of which are presented in Box 6.

BOX 6

FUQUA'S TRAINING PROGRAMME

THE FUQUA PROGRAMME FOR CIS MANAGER DEVELOPMENT AND CORPORATE INTERNSHIP

1. The Centre for former USSR Manager Development began in spring 1990 through a USD 4 million gift from J.B. Fuqua, Senior Chairman of the Board, Fuqua Industries. Although the programme it offers is distinct, it is nevertheless typical of many new courses being offered by US business schools to eastern European managers in general, and former Soviet managers in particular.

The training programme

2. The Training Programme is offered twice a year to a group of 35-45 CIS managers for a four week period.

Week 1 is devoted to a basic grounding in the functioning of market economies. On day 1 students are given instruction in the market economy (industry structure, pricing role of Governments, role of profits), and on the second and third day market-based management comprising of the role of marketing, marketing decisions (product, price, promotion and distribution), customer segmentation and competitive positioning. On day 4 students visit a factory to see United States management in practice. On the fifth day, students attend a course on capital markets - banking systems, stock markets, bond markets and corporate financial policy.

BOX 6 (Continued)

In **Week 2** students receive instruction on technology management covering - manufacturing strategy, matching product and process, project planning, total quality management and production and operation management - and human resources management - strategy, employee involvement, team building, industrial relations and trade unions. Two days are also assigned for computer simulation exercises designed to show how U.S. firms make decisions about R & D, production, marketing, pricing, etc.

Week 3 focuses on the impact of economic reform on management: studying methods of privatization, creating new businesses and developing products for western markets. In **Week 4**, the Soviet student becomes an intern in a United States company.

Selection of candidates and the role of United States firms

3. Candidates for the course (average age 35 - 45 years) are directors, deputy directors or chief engineers of industrial plants. Initial selection is carried out by the Academy of National Economy in Moscow and by the Fuqua School which reserves the right to make the final decision with regard to the composition of each group. Priority is accorded to managers in industrial sectors of interest to US firms.

Knowledge of English, while desirable, is not critical; simultaneous translation for course work is provided.

US firms participate in this programme in a number of ways:

- by sending their Soviet joint venture managers to the three-week course and by sponsoring candidates for the one-week internship. The company pays part of the cost of the course and the cost of the internship;

- by nominating a current or potential Soviet partner or customer. Here the US firm covers the cost of the internship;

- by "hosting" a Soviet manager from a relevant industrial sector. The manager would initially be selected by the school but the sponsoring firm would cover the costs of the one-week internship.

Goals of the programme

4. The aim of the programme falls into two broad categories: first, to teach the former Soviet manager about the market economy; demonstrate the style, techniques and methods of US management ; and as an interne, to see first-hand how his joint venture partner's company works. Second, to give to United States firms the opportunity to learn from Soviet industrial managers and directors about business prospects in a relatively unknown market and to build contacts with these managers for future business activities.

Doubts have been voiced, however, about the effectiveness of these standard courses for training managers for joint ventures. Generally, these doubts refer to:

- their short duration (some are so short, it is claimed, that they give the trainee little more than a notion of the training establishment);

- their one-off nature (follow-up courses arranged after the trainee has had the opportunity to put what they have learned into practice, generally are recognized to be more useful);

- the unpreparedness of the trainee (often lacking basic linguistic skills);

- the use of western management concepts without proper background explanation - quality control, cash flow etc., - as well the use of the standard market economy categories - production, marketing, finance etc. which mean little to managers trained in centrally planned economies;

- the exclusive focus on the training of senior managers, thus ignoring the needs at lower management levels;

- their academic nature (many courses are designed to teach eastern European managers about the host country's management system- American, French etc., rather than to train the student in the specific skills they will require as managers).

There is a widespread recognition, too, that factors hampering the ability of western management schools to address the needs of eastern European managers are:

- the lack of programmes, materials, case-studies which are jointly designed and researched by eastern and western management training specialists;

- the lack of training programmes which cater for mixed (East and West) management groups.

- the general lack of funds to develop these efforts.

Consequently, as a result of this experience, there has been tendency for western business schools to change their approach to the management problem in eastern Europe and to move away from these short-term standard courses to other activities which better reflect their own institutional strengths and expertise.

Two activities, in particular, are now being emphasised. Firstly whilst still providing courses in the West, western management schools are refocussing these exclusively for the top level managers of East-West joint ventures and on the specific needs and goals of the joint- venture. Secondly, western business schools are increasingly looking to establishing institutional links with management schools in the East to assist large western corporations organize their management training activities in co- operation with local East European management schools. Under such an arrangement, funded principally by the corporation, the western management school will recruit and train local teachers, work out syllabi and provide organizational assistance. In this way, western management schools would become brokers between large firms seeking a pool of local managers at all levels and the local training centres. Examples of this new strategy are becoming frequent.

(2) Training the trainers

Courses run for the trainers of management schools in eastern Europe have become an increasingly popular way in which the western business school can assist the training of managers in the region, although all the main projects are still in their early stages of development.

IMD, INSEAD, London Business School, Consortium

A consortium of leading business schools (London Business School, IMD Lausanne, and INSEAD Fontainebleau) in Europe has been recently established to design "training the trainer" programmes for eastern Europe. The programme, which is going to be held in the West, will consist of a four week academic programme, a three week practical period involving participating firms -with a one week wrap-up. The target is to involve 40 participants each time: two groups from central and eastern Europe, and one group from the former Soviet Union, alternating annually. The programme is proposed to be held three times a year, the first starting in the summer of 1992.

International Faculty Development Programme (IFDP)

The IFDP is a programme devised by Instituto de Estudios Superiores de la Empresa (Spain), SDA- Bocconi (Italy) and ISA-HEC (France) to train business educators from central and eastern European countries. Starting in October 1992, it plans to annually train 100 central and eastern European professors of management annually. The programme will primarily benefit participating management schools in central and eastern Europe whose staff will come to the three western schools for training.

The eastern management institutions that are currently forming the European network are the following:

1. International School of Commerce in Rynia (Poland)
2. Budapest University of Economic Sciences (Hungary)
3. Higher Commercial Management School of the Ministry of Foreign Economic Relations (Moscow)
4. The Graduate School of International Business of Academy of National Economy (Moscow)
5. International Business School of Moscow State Institute of International Relations
6. International Management Institute SP - ST.Petersburg - (former LIMI)
7. Warsaw University of Technology
8. School of Management, Warsaw University
9. International Executive Development Centre
10. Prague School of Economics
11. Bratislava School of Economics
12. Sofia University
13. Central School of Commerce (SGH)
14. Lódz University

The United States programme

On the North American continent, five of the most prestigious business schools (Harvard, Wharton, MIT, Stanford and Northwestern) have established a similar programme to begin the summer of 1992 with a proposed first year in take of 100-120 students. This Program will comprise four distinct parts over 1-2 years. Part 1 in the home country, will include home studies in areas of accounting, marketing and English. Part 2 in the USA, with the general management programme of 5-12 weeks at either one of the 5 schools. Part 3 again in the home country, includes a field case study. In the final part in the USA again, the participants will be able to specialize in one of six management fields at either of the five schools, for a period of 6 weeks.

The advantage of having a "training the trainers" programme is that it maximizes the contribution of western business schools to building up local management development capabilities and thus to raising management standards in eastern Europe. On the other hand, training specialists point out that the transferries of the necessary skills from one trainer to another cannot be effectively done in the space of a four weeks but requires long-term contacts between the teacher and student involving collaboration in teaching and research.

4.3 MAJOR MANAGEMENT DEVELOPMENT PROBLEMS

Western firms investigating the quality of management training schools in eastern Europe with a view to either sending for training, or recruiting managers will discover that they are not starved of choice. In the last four years new "private" management schools have proliferated everywhere in eastern Europe. However, with a few notable exceptions these new establishments are doing little to raise overall standards in eastern European management.

In the CIS for example recent advertisements in the press for new management programmes reveal that:

- almost all the courses are offered for a duration of between 1 and 4 months and appear rather short to obtain the results promised, e.g. three week courses on how to become an "entrepreneur". In some cases the courses are especially brief (e.g. establishing a joint venture (25 hours); marketing and advertising (50 hours).

- there is an emphasis on marketing and foreign trade activities rather than on management per se, reflecting the fact that the main catalyst for these establishments of many of those institutes was the decree of 1989 extending the right to state enterprises to conduct their own import-export operations;

- the cost of all of these courses - and particularly those involving short-term study at a management training institute in the West is very high (the cost, for example, of attending a 4 week course in the United States was the equivalent to 500 times the average Soviet annual wage);

- the courses offered class room education; no practical managerial training.

It can therefore be argued that creating an adequate management training resource will not be done overnight:

First, in all the economies in transition business education programmes have only limited support from Governments. The latter are hard pressed to produce quick and spectacular improvements and thus have been reluctant to devote resources to areas which can only give long-term results. In addition, there may well be a cultural legacy from the old system which tended to view non-material, service-oriented activities in eastern economies as non-productive. Finally the underfunding of education is due to budget deficits and the search for immediate savings as explained in Section I. For example, the dramatic cuts in education funding at all levels in September-October 1991 in Poland, to reduce the budget deficit are a good indication that it may take time before the governments of these countries appreciate the long-term, intangible effects of such investments.

Second, the number of qualified and experienced lecturers is rather limited in the eastern Europe. The growing number of public and private business schools (about 30 were in operation in Poland at the end of 1991, although many were just barely functioning) reflects primarily personal ambition and fashion. Most of them will not grow because they lack teaching materials, a stable faculty, international contacts and infrastructure. In Poland, for example, most new schools run courses in rented facilities. The education gap cannot be easily closed with western teachers coming for a short period of time to deliver lectures. The effort to train educators abroad (in the USA and Europe) undertaken with the help of foreign governments, will eventually bring positive results, but as previously mentioned will have its impact only in the long-term.

Third and paradoxically, the demand for economic and business education is rather limited and sporadic. The recent experiences of two well-established business schools in Warsaw are anecdotal, but worth mentioning. The International Business School S.A., created as the second private business school in 1989, was, in September 1991, enroling candidates for its third two-year, part-time, postgraduate MBA course, and the Polish International School of Business was offering executives a part-time, four month course. Despite heavy promotion and advertising in the domestic press, radio and even TV, the number of applicants in both school was relatively small: about 80 applicants in each school.

Overall, a short time frame dominates the attitude of government officials, private businessmen and managers of state-owned firms in eastern Europe. Governments will have to deflect the current demand for short courses and instant recipes on how to deal with business contingencies and help build more lasting management training systems around a longer-term perspective.

A new more practical approach to management training is needed in the economies in transition. As set out in Box 7 there is a need to switch the emphasis from teaching management to learning management by doing and from institute based learning to company based learning. The role of trainer, too, needs to be reassessed in the light of the new goals and previous practice. Students must be provided with more opportunities to participate in their teaching rather than be "spoon fed" by the teacher as in the past. Programmes, too, must be adapted to practical needs not to abstract theories. They should be tailor-made and so designed as to achieve specific objectives. Wherever possible training should be integrated into the objectives of companies. Here the value of using company case studies in teaching management courses should be stressed.

```
┌─────────────────────────────────────────────────────────────┐
│                          BOX 7                               │
│          CHANGES REQUIRED IN TRAINING APPROACH               │
├──────────────────────────────┬──────────────────────────────┤
│           F R O M            │            T O               │
├──────────────────────────────┼──────────────────────────────┤
│                              │   Management Development     │
│      Teaching Process        │   Management Consulting and  │
│                              │      Action Learning         │
├──────────────────────────────┼──────────────────────────────┤
│   Institute-Based Teaching   │   Company-Based Learning     │
├──────────────────────────────┼──────────────────────────────┤
│                              │  Learner-Controlled Learning,│
│  Trainer-Controlled Teaching │       Self-Development       │
├──────────────────────────────┼──────────────────────────────┤
│                              │        Tailor-made,          │
│    Standardized programme    │ Result-Oriented training Systems│
├──────────────────────────────┼──────────────────────────────┤
│     Fragmented Training      │ Integrated into Company objectives Training│
└──────────────────────────────┴──────────────────────────────┘
```

Source: Joseph Prokopenko, "Human Resources Management in Economics in Transition: The East European Case", Man Dev/66, ILO, 1992.

4.4. MANAGEMENT DEVELOPMENT INSTITUTIONAL MECHANISMS AND SELECTED PROGRAMMES

To encourage the development of contacts between western business and management training institutes in eastern and western countries the following section provides information on management schools which are active in the field of training eastern European managers. Wherever possible the name of the Director of the programme, the address, fax and telephone number of the institute, the nature of the programme, the links the institute has with other schools and the source of funding for these programmes, is given. The information supplied is based on a questionnaire survey carried out by the Economic Commission for Europe (ECE) of 200 training institutes in eastern and western Europe and the United States of America and Canada between October 1991 and February 1992.

Only those schools which provide training programmes for managers of East-West joint ventures and for eastern European managers generally were selected to be published in this Guide.

AUSTRIA

Hernstein International Management Institute (HIMI)

Berggasse 16, A-1092 Wien.
Tel: (0222) 345 611-0
Fax: (0222) 345 611-17

*Experience

The HIMI was founded in 1966 as a Vienna Chamber of Commerce venture, specializing in management training, and have had experience with management training for East European managers since 1986 in Hungary, and since 1988 in Soviet Union, Czechoslovakia and Yugoslavia.

*Programmes

The HIMI does not run any standard programmes, but rather tries to tailor-make programmes in order to fit the clients specific goals and needs for the venture. The structure of the programmes that are offered include: train the trainer programmes; training services for top managers and tailor-made in-company training. There is an emphasis on the "medium to long-term" length of courses, which are being held in both Austria and in the eastern European countries.

*Funding

The HIMI are sponsored by the Vienna Chamber of Commerce, to which the student can also apply for financing. The student can also get funding from, for instance, the World Bank and the Federal Chamber of Commerce.

....

Ost West Akademie für Management und Marketing (OWA)

Director: Mag. Elke Schildberger
Wiener Straße 131, A-4020 Linz.
Tel: (0732) 493 51-520
Fax: (0732) 493 58

*Experience

The OWA was established in 1989 to try and meet the demand for specialized training on management as eastern Europe began the move to a market economy. The OWA's target group is both eastern and western managers. OWA has joined forces with institutes in the Commonwealth of Independent States - Moscow International Business School - MIRBIS; International Research Institute for Management Sciences - IRIMS -, in Poland - University of Ljublin; Foreign Trade Institute - Warsaw -, the Hungarian Chamber of Commerce, Bulgaria, and the Czech and Slovak Federal Republic.

*Programmes	There are three types of programmes offered in 1991/92. These include: basic seminars, special projects and a post graduate programme. A "standard basic seminars" programme will last approximately 12 days and include: lectures on chosen topics (e.g. marketing, controlling) held by business practitioners with experience of eastern Europe; a 4-day business game; and different company visits. Typically, 10-20 participants from a targeted eastern Europe country will participate. "Special projects" will typically last 2-3 days and include business forums, tailor-made seminars, and discussion groups. Finally, there is a post graduate programme given in co-operation with the University of Linz. This programme lasts 15 weeks and includes lectures on finance, accounting, marketing and organizational theory.

....

Department of Small Business Management
(Vienna University of Economics)

Prof. Josef Mugler
University of Economics, Augasse 2-6, A-1090 Vienna
Tel: (0222) 31 336 45 92
Fax: (0222) 31 336 715

*Programme	The Department of Small Business Management of the Vienna University of Economics is offering a two-week course for university teachers from the reforming countries in central and eastern Europe in German from 5 to 18 July 1992. The programme aims at developing a course curriculum for universities and business schools in the field of small business economics and management. The programme is open to 25 participants who will receive a scholarship from the Austrian Government covering the costs or registration and their subsistence.

....

Projektmanagement Austria-Institut (PMA)
(an der Wirtschaftsuniversität Wien)

Directors of Programme: Karl Volonte and Günter Rattay
Franz Klein-Gasse 1, A-1190 Wien
Tel: (0222) 347 641 / 215-217
Fax: (0222) 319 785 5

*Experience	The PMA is a non-profit institute specializing in professional project management. PMA has developed close links with national project management associations in 18 European countries in both western and eastern Europe. PMA is specifically set up to provide skills for Austrian, Czech and Hungarian managers of business oriented organizations who are getting involved in joint projects. Partners of the PMA includes: Ministry of Economic Policy and Development of CSFR; Agency for Foreign Investors; the Hungarian and the CSFR Project management Association.

*Programmes	The PMA runs 20 four-day seminars and a few symposia a year. A considerable practical emphasis is placed by PMA to its training seminars, so that skills transferred can be immediately used. Furthermore, the first steps of the actual joint project will be performed within the seminar itself. Teaching is in German. Interpreters are available.
*Funding	A few participants will be sent by the INTERNET, CSFR and the Ministry of Economic Policy and Development of the CSFR. The Austrian sponsor is the Ministry for Economic Affairs.

BELGIUM

Management Centre Europe (MCE)
(The European Headquarters of the American Management Association International)

Programme Director: Wolfgang Lux
Rue Caroly, 15, B-1040 Brussels, Belgium

*Programmes
  and
  activities

MCE's activities in central and eastern Europe involve:

- the organization of seminars for western executives informing them about developments in these markets and emerging opportunities. Seminars have been organized thus far on the former Soviet Union, Czech and Slovak Federal Republic and the former GDR.

- providing the standard MCE course to local managers in partnership with local organizations in Moscow and Prague. So far the emphasis has been on basic skill courses, such as the fundamentals of Finance and Strategic Planning.

- the development of in-company programmes in conjunction with Czech and Slovak partners, to train managers of joint ventures active in the region.

BULGARIA

Institute of Management and Administration

Director of programme: Professor Evka Razvigorova
21 Poinerski pqt, 1635 Sofia, Bulgaria
Tel: 56 69 15
Fax: 859 25 22 189
Telex: 22 832

*Programmes   Seminars to help both eastern and western managers create and manage East-West joint ventures are being organized by Professor Evka Razvigorova at the Institute of Management and Administration, Sofia, Bulgaria. These seminars will examine Bulgarian investment and trade laws, the procedures for developing and creating joint ventures and certain operational problems affecting joint ventures in Bulgaria. Further information about these seminars, which are given both in English and in Bulgarian can be obtained from the above-mentioned address.

....

University of National and World Economics (UNWE)

Director of Programme: Dr. George Kalushev
Management Department, 38 Slavinska St., 1000 Sofia
Tel: 681 514 / 875 820
Fax: 681 514

*Experience   The management department of the UNWE has been running undergraduate and postgraduate programmes in the fields of business organization and management for the past two decades. For the most part these courses were designed for a socio-economic environment which no longer exists in the country.

*Programmes   Since 1991 the University joined with the University of Arizona (TUCSON) and the Polytechnic of West London to introduce new curricula in business administration and management. Deserving particular mention is a programme which will be starting in September 1992, called an "Open Learning Programme in Business Studies" tailor-made for Bulgaria and designed for participants with relevant work-experience. It aims at being very practice oriented, providing basic western-type business education. Given the role of the Polytechnic of West London in the design of the programme, the United Kingdom Commission for National Academic Awards have fully accredited it.

*Funding   Tuition fee based.

THE COMMONWEALTH OF INDEPENDENT STATES

International Business School (IBS)
(Moscow State Institute of International Relations, Ministry of Foreign Affairs)

Director General: Mr. Andrei Manoukovsky
76, prosp. Vernadskogo, 117454 Moscow
Tel: (095) 434 9253
Fax: (095) 434 0160

*Experience and activities	IBS is associated with the Moscow State Institute of International Relations and the USSR Ministry of Foreign Affairs. During 1990/91 the IBS has been a co-organizer of a number of international conferences and workshops:

- "Negotiating joint venture agreements", 19-23 March 1991 with the United Nations Centre on Transactional Corporations.
- "Security Markets in the Market Economy", with Salomon Brothers Inc. 3-8 December 1990.
- "Transaction to Economic and Social Democracy" with Harvard University and the Moscow City Council, 16-18 April 1991.

*Programmes   The school offers:

- post graduate education to Soviet middle-to-top managers.
- an introduction to the Soviet market for foreign companies.
- research, and consultancies to foreign firms.

*Funding   State funding and private sponsors.

....

International Management Institute, Kiev (IMI)

54/1, prosp. Peremohy, 252057 Kiev - Ukraine
Tel: (044) 446 2451 / 86
Fax: (044) 446 2447

*Experience   IMI was established in 1989 as a joint venture between the Academy of Sciences of Ukraine and the IMI Geneva (now IMD-Lausanne). It was created with a mission to develop leaders in governments, commerce and industry who will expand opportunities for international trade and co-operation. IMI has a staff of 40, where 2 are full-time foreign professional. About 20 foreign specialists spends up to several months doing research and teaching at IMI.

*Programmes	IMI offers a one year MBA programme, and from this year (1992) also a two year MBA, which will be offered jointly with Fordham University, New York. The one year programme is intended for young managers and administrators with a minimum of 2 years experience, and is designed to international standards. It includes learning a foreign business language and a 2-month internship in a business abroad. IMI offers also 1 and 3-month executive programmes.
*Funding	Funding comes from tuition fees, the Academy of Sciences of Ukraine and from several western companies and foundations.

....

International Management Institute of St. Petersburg (IMISP)

Director: Mr. Sergey Mordovin
P.O. Box 450, 199034 St. Petersburg
Tel: 007 812 256 7113
Fax: 007 812 218 0402

*Experience	IMISP, former Leningrad Institute of Management, was formed through the initiative of the Italian SDA-Bocconi school in 1989. IMISP draws resources from a pool of European and US business schools.
*Programmes	The IMISP intends to run an MBA course tailored to the needs of managers approaching a market economy, which is being designed in conjunction with ESC-Lyon, Henley Management College (UK), ERASMUS University in Rotterdam and ESADE Business School of Barcelona. It focuses also on organizing seminars and work shops for both foreign and domestic managers. In December 1991 the School moved to its new headquarters at the recently refurbished Smolny Ministry. Facilities include a business library and a computer room.
*Funding	The MBA project has been approved for funding by the European Community.

....

Leti - St Petersburg Elektrotechnical Institute and Louvain University, Belgium

*Programmes	School offers MBA programme for graduates of engineering school. Graduates receive a LETI-Louvain MBA certificate.

....

Moscow International Business School (MIRBIS)

Director: Mr. Stanislav Savin
Tel: 237 9220 / 237 3430
Fax: (7-095) 257 34 30
Telex: 412 110 MIRBIS SU

*Experience	MIRBIS was opened in the beginning of 1989 as a joint venture operation between the G.V. Plekhanov Moscow Institute of Economics and the Italian economic research company Nomizma. This was the first business school in the Soviet Union. The school has established links with prestigious western business schools in both Europe and the US. Courses are being read by noted Soviet and foreign economists, and are aimed at Soviet managers in private as well as public sectors.
*Programmes	Three programmes are offered at the moment: "Master"; "Mirbis"; and "Top Manager". The first is a MBA-style one-year course which includes training in a foreign company or administrative body abroad. Teaching is done by means of lectures, seminars and business games. An English language course of Cambridge University is included. Graduates are awarded a diploma. The second is an one-month intensive course, which includes a 10 day training programme in an Italian firm. The third course offered, is a 10-day intensive course, in part or in full, abroad. MIRBIS also offers a special programme for retired army officers (6months) and a longer one (9months) in public relations.
*Funding	Students pay tuition fees one part in foreign and the other in local currency.

....

Higher Commercial Management School (HCMS)

32 Levoberejanaya ul., 125475 Moscow
Tel: (095) 458 6012 or (095) 458 9606
Fax: (095) 200 2205
Telex: 411 162 HCMS

*Programmes	HCMS offers intensive 8 week courses in the USSR and a 3-4 weeks internships abroad. Basic courses are in motivational management; marketing; advertising; computer-aided accounting; commercial bank operations; stock market and other. The specialized courses deal with management in business, small enterprise and entrepreneurship. A business English language course gives the opportunity of obtaining the London Chamber of Commerce and Industry certificate (diploma).

....

Moscow State University School of Business (founded: 1989)

Director: Mr. Oteg S. Vikhansky
Tel: (7-095) 939 37 24
Fax: (7-095) 939 08 77

*Programmes	The school provides three courses: a two month course for directors of state enterprises; a 10 week course for small business managers; and an MBA programme established in 1993.

....

Higher School of International Business of the Academy of National Economy

Rector: Mr. L.I. Evenko
82 Prospekt Vernadskogo, 117571 Moscow
Tel: (095) 434 11 46 or (095) 434 83 89
Fax: (095) 433 25 65 or 420 20 65 or 420 22 66
Telex: 411 626 KARTU SU

*Programmes   HSIB offers business courses of 4 to 8 weeks including an internship abroad. Basis courses cover organization of business operations abroad, establishment and management of a joint venture; marketing; conversion of defence industries. The specialized courses deal with the programmes of local self-administration; new forms of economic activity; organization of free economic zones. An English language course is offered which is accredited by the Californian University Business School.

THE CZECH REPUBLIC

The Czech Management Centre (CMC)

nám.5.kvetna 2
250 88 Celakovice.
Tel: 42-202-91-441
Fax: 42-202-91-997

*Experience   CMC was founded in 1990 in Prague as a foundation. The co-founders are the President of the University of Pittsburgh and the Czech Minister of Industry.

*Programmes   CMC offers a one-year MBA course to international standard. This is an executive education for senior and middle managers, which includes an internship programme for executives in western firms. The programme emphasises the teaching of practical skills, and is specifically geared to East and central European issues.Successful participants gets a CMC Certificate and credits for a western university.

*Funding   The studies at CMC are self-financed. Main contributors to the foundation has been the Czech and Slovak State Bank; the Commercial Bank of Czechoslovakia and the Ministry of Industry for the Czech Republic. Others include the Rockefeller Brothers Fund, University of Pittsburgh and the Milan Chamber of Commerce.

European Business School-Prague (EBS-P)

Sokolovska 278
18044 Prague 9
Czech Republic
Tel: (0042) 02/265 243
Fax: (0042) 02/236 6373

*Experience   The school was established in early 1990 as a joint venture between European Business School in Germany (see separate section) and the Czechoslovakian government, and is associated with EBS in London, Parma and Budapest. The academic management is held by the German outfit, in co-operation with the International Institute for Law and Management. EBS also cooperates with universities in Phoenix and San Diego USA, and has similar arrangements with universities in both France and Buenos Aires.

*Programmes   The one-year programme is targeted at senior executives who are given a general management course, including a period of work experience in German companies. The object is to familiarize Czechoslovakian executives with the general framework and economic policy instruments of a "social market economy". At request, specially tailored programmes for enterprises, etc. can be developed.

*Funding   There is a current (1991) restructuring of the operation, to form a company called EBS-Eastern Europe Ltd. When the first 90 executives graduated in June 1991, the funding was based on tuition fees, donations from companies, and scholarships from the German Foreign Ministry.

....

Vysoká skola ekonomická

Rektorát: Prof. Ing. Milan Maly, CSc
Nám. W. Churchilla 4
130 67 Praha 3
Czech Republic
Fax: (0042-2) 235 45 61

*Programmes   Within the University, the Institute for Consulting and Economic Expertise offers two courses for business managers in joint ventures:

- dealing with foreign firms in joint venture relationships

- on western management methods for managing in a transition economy.

Lectures are conducted in Czech but the faculty are also able to offer courses in English and German.

FRANCE

The European Centre for Entrepreneurship (ECE)

Managing Director: Mr. Didier Loing
P.O. Box 183, 68004 Colmar Cedex
Tel: 0033 892 393 43
Fax: 0033 892 390 31

*Programmes ECE has a three week consortium programme: European Entrepreneurship Programme (EEP), designed to advance entrepreneurial competence. It includes aspects of the emerging new Europe and deals with the new business opportunities in eastern Europe. ECE also offers Intra-company workshops specially designed to meet requirements. Both programmes are conducted in English.

....

European Institute of Business Administration (INSEAD)

Boulv. de Constance, 77305 Fontainebleau Cedex
Tel: (1) 607 240 00
Fax: (1) 607 242 42

*Experience INSEAD was established in 1959, and has grown to become one of the leading business schools in the world.

*Programmes INSEAD does not run regular East European management programmes. It runs a 1-year MBA as well as executive, company specific programmes. A 4-week Advanced Management Programme Eastern Europe was held in 1991, designed for managers from the former GDR. Teaching was conducted by means of case studies, apparently with a considerable emphasis on practical skills. The school is currently taking part in a joint consortium between itself, IMD and LBS, to develop a train the trainer programme.

*Funding Sponsors included: ABB, BASF, Lufthansa, Thyssen, Volkswagen and Varta. 15 former GDR managers were fully sponsored.

GERMANY

Institut für Umweltschutz (INFU)

Head of Section: Dipl.Ing. Hans-Peter Winkelmann
Universität Dortmund, Postfach 500500,
4600 Dortmund
Tel: (49-231) 755 4096
Fax: (49-231) 755 4084

*Programme   The Institute is currently preparing a training course for managers of the
                  industrial-military complex of the CIS with emphasis on environment
                  management.

Die Akademie für Führungskräfte der Wirtschaft (AFW)

Managing Director: Norbert A. Klis
Postfach 1116, 3388 Bad Harzburg 1.
Tel: (05322) 730
Fax: (05322) 7324.

*Experience   Founded in 1959 the AFW was one of the first privately owned and operated
                  companies dealing with Continued Education for Management in the former
                  GDR and the East European countries, especially the former Soviet Union.

*Programmes   The AFW is continuously training Russian, Polish and Ukrainian top-level
                  managers. AFW programmes are tailor-made for client firms and associations
                  of the chemical and petro-chemical industry, agriculture and foreign trade.
                  Seminars run typically for 6-7 days and are held in Russian and German. The
                  seminars take place in Germany as well as in eastern European countries.
                  AFW holds 600 seminars a year on 110 topics.

*Funding   The AFW is a subsidiary of the German enterprise, Cognus AG, Hamburg,
                  and is registered as a private limited company.

Deutsches Institut für Betriebswirtschaft e.V. (DIB)

Director : Dipl.-Volksw. Wolfgang Werner
Postfach 101139, 6000 Frankfurt 1.
Tel: (069) 219 7245
Fax: (069) 219 7424

*Programmes   DIB provides seminars and training for all kinds of economic requirements in
                  industry, trade and administration. These mainly consists of seminars lasting

for 1-2 days on special questions in economics. DIB are also offering "in-house-training" for enterprises tailored to the need of costumers.

*Funding N.A. Private clients.

....

Institut für Datenverarbeitung und Betriebswirtschaft Consult (IDB)

Rainbow Center, Klein Seligenstädter Grund 11, D-6056 Hensenstamm
Tel: 061 046 997 - 55
Fax: 061 046 997 - 56

*Experience IDB have for 20 years been involved in the teaching of business and computer sciences. IDB has representative offices in Tallin (Estonia), Moscow (Russia), as well as established offices in the former GDR.

*Programmes IDB has practical experience of devising study programmes geared to the problems of transition from planned to market economy. The programmes, generally in forms of special seminars, are held both in Germany and in the eastern countries. IDB teachers are fluent in English, German and Russian and courses are given in all three languages.

*Funding IDB is a private limited company.

....

Institut für Management und Technologie (IMT)

Director: Prof.Dr.-ing. Günther Seliger
Ehrenbergstraße 29, D-1000 Berlin 33 (Dahlen)
Tel: 030 831 8061
Fax: 030 831 8067

*Experience IMT is an educational institute used by large corporations, which cooperates with universities and institutions in the area. It is involved in the conversion of military industries to civilian uses and enterprise restructuring, especially in Russia.

*Programmes The IMT Berlin is a training facility for the upper management of industrial companies. The main focus is on the search for integrative solutions of combined technical and economical problems. The institute's approach cover a wide range of activities from seminars on Global Production Strategies in the GUS to specific management training programmes for industrial managers from eastern Europe. The IMT has in 1992 completed a East-West Forum in Berlin, where 35 Russian Entrepreneurs made a presentation of their companies, products and aims for cooperation with foreign companies to more than 350 German participants.

*Funding IMT is a private limited company.

....

Internationales Institut für Recht und Unternehmensführung an der EBS (IRU)

Schloss Reichartshausen, 6227 Oestrich-Winkel.
Tel: (06723) 691 09
Fax: (06723) 306 4

*Experience   IRU is a private institute of sciences within the European Business School
                  (EBS) association, which is comprised of the EBS in Germany at Schloss
                  Reichartshausen, London, Parma, Prague and Budapest (See separate sections).

*Programmes   The aim of the institute is to provide information on management practice and
                  general management by means of offering a generalist education together with
                  work experience in German companies. Duration is 1-year.

*Funding   IRU is a private limited company.

....

Industrie- und Handelskammer zu Köln (IHK)

Postfach 108015, 5000 Cologne 1.
Tel: (0221) 164 00
Fax: (0221) 164 0123

*Programmes   IHK gives seminars on economic and business relations, with an emphasis on
                  exporting to other countries. Some seminars cover countries in eastern and
                  central Europe, the duration of which generally are between 1-2 days. They
                  also offer "compact study courses" - "exportpraxis", with an IHK certificate,
                  but with no special emphasis on eastern Europe relations.

*Funding   Participants pay seminar fees.

NETHERLANDS

Cap Gemini Pandata, Institute of Informatics (CGPII)

P.O. Box 3164, 3502 GD Utrecht.
Tel: (309) 294 40
Fax: (309) 333 42

*Experience   Totally 267 branches are represented by the CGPII organization, in Europe as
                  well as in the USA.

*Programmes	CGPII is a software services and consultancy group, as well as an institute of training which gives advice on projects to central and eastern Europe. They offer tailor made programmes and train the trainer courses towards specialists involved in automation and information management. Duration of programmes are "longer-term".
*Funding	Privately funded.

HUNGARY

European Business School -Budapest (EBS-B)

Hajos u 25, 1065 Budapest.
Tel: 132 8377
Fax: 111 5054

*Experience	EBS-B was founded in 1991 as a joint venture between the European Business School Schloss Reichartshausen, 6227 Oestrich-Winkel, Germany, and a foundation for the promotion of EBS-Hungary, consisting of 15 Hungarian companies. (See sections: Germany, Czechoslovakia).

....

International Management Centre (IMC)

Pentz Karoly u 1-3, 1221 Budapest XXII.
Tel: (226) 5128 / 0755
Fax: (226) 5340

*Objectives IMC was founded in 1988 as the first private business school in eastern Europe with the following objectives:

1. to promote the use of market economy management skills and western know-how to enhance Hungary's position as an effective and responsible participant in international business.

2. to promote the spread of business management as a profession and of a new type of business and management culture and to strengthen its status in Hungary.

To accomplish these goals IMC has developed a wide international network of professional assistance and cooperation through its members and Advisory Board members as well as through its links with such universities as:

University of Pittsburgh (USA), York University (Can), Indiana University (USA), IMD (Switzerland), Manchester Business School (UK), INSEAD (France), Tulane University (New Orleans) and the Nijerode School of Business (Breukelen, Netherlands).

*Programmes

1. The Young Manager Programme, which is a 12 month post-graduate programme for future managers. Towards the end of the programme, the students take part in a 6-12 week internship at a western company. At the conclusion of the programme they receive a certificate. They can then enter the MBA programme at the University of Pittsburgh or at other degree-granting institutions.

2. Executive Education programmes for senior and middle managers. These short courses present the theoretical knowledge and practical skills needed to participate in market economies on an international scale.

3. Consulting services for companies faced with making decisions on strategy and policy changes, restructuring or other important business matters.

YMP candidates should be between the ages of 25 and 35, professionally qualified managers with a good knowledge of English. Applicants are strictly screened by an admission committee consisting of foreign and Hungarian professors, successful managers and programme alumni. IMC selects the 25-30 best qualified to start their studies together. In 1991 students on the YMP came from Austria, Germany, Romania, USA as well as Hungary. Curriculum for the YMP was designed jointly by IMC and the University of Pittsburgh and taught entirely in English.

*Funding

Sponsors of the institute are western firms and universities, as well as private foundations. Western firms sponsor students during the internship period on the YMP course.

....

East-West Management Institute International (EWMI)

Executive Director: Zsuzsanna Ránki, M.B.A. (Indiana University)
Szent Istvan Krt.4, 1137 Budapest.
Tel: (36-1) 132 5642
Fax: (36-1) 132 5642

*Experience
and objectives

The main purpose of EWNI is to arrange internship programmes for professionals from central and eastern Europe in order to assist in opening up and developing the business and management environment in this region. EWMI has affiliated offices throughout the former Soviet Union, central and eastern Europe, London and Washington.

*Programmes

EWNI is establishing a fully computerized database of those individuals who have applied for an internship with a foreign company. The database may be accessed through EWNI by the organizations interested in providing internship opportunities.

A multi-level search process, specially designed for this purpose matches candidates with the host organization's specifications. Once EWNI identifies possible candidates for a placement with a foreign firm, it assists the host organization in screening candidates in order that the most capable are selected.

EWNI also runs an intensive four week management and language orientation programme for the selected candidates, after which the finalists may start their internship.

*Funding EWNI administrative costs are underwritten by philanthropist and Wall Street financier, George Soros. The firm which hosts an intern is expected to pay directly to each a stipend for living expenses, provide housing and pay for travel. The host companies also are expected to contribute a nominal fee to the EWNI's overhead expenses.

....

Technical University of Budapest (TUB)
(Department of Industrial Management and Economics)

Muegyetem rkp. 9. T. ep., H-1502 Budapest XI.
Tel: (36-1) 166 5211 / 24-32
Fax: (36-1) 166 5208

*Programmes The Technical University of Budapest in co-operation with the Heriot-Watt University Business School, Edinburgh, United Kingdom, is launching a part-time MBA. Programme in English, starting in September 1992.

The International Master of Business Administration Programme is designed to develop professional and entrepreneurial management skills to meet the challenges of the future. The degree is fully recognized internationally as a business diploma.

According to the University participants can build new personal relationships, learn from each others' experiences, while acquiring a wide range of managerial skills. This objective will be achieved by the teaching staff supported by and under the supervision of the faculty of the Heriot-Watt University.

Course requirements:

- applicants for the programme must hold a degree in engineering or equivalent qualification.
- have at least two years work experience.
- must pass: the Graduate Management Test with a score of 500; and the Test of English as a Foreign Language with a score of 500.

Entry to the MBA programme is by competition.

Classes will be taught by lecturers from the Technical University and other Hungarian Universities with Visiting Professors from Heriot-Watt. In addition, experienced practitioners from Industry and Commerce will cover certain subjects.

*Funding   The part-time course will cost 160,000 Hungarian Forint per semester.

ITALY

SDA Bocconi Scoula di Direzione Aziendale Dell' Universita Liugi Bocconi

Via F. Bocconi 8, 20136 Milano
Tel: +392 894 010 84
Fax: +392 894 082 63

*Experience   SDA is considered to be one of Europe's leading business schools.

*Programmes   SDA established a joint venture between itself and the International Management Institute in St. Petersburg in 1989 (see separate section under the Commonwealth).

LATVIA

Higher Management School

10 GSP b. Kommunaru, 226150 Riga
Tel: 32 5320

*Experience   HMS was established under the auspices of the Latvian Institute of Higher Managers - specialists in the national economy.

*Programmes	HMS offers a 2-year training course intended for managers with higher education from the state and private sectors. It covers management, economics, marketing, foreign economic relations, business culture, psychology and inter-personal communication, computer training and business English. An internship in a business abroad is included in the curriculum. The graduates obtain a second diploma of higher education.
*Funding	The tuition fee was 8950 roubles in 1991. Students are provided with accommodations in Riga.

POLAND

The Jagiellonian University (JU)

Director: Dr Hab Janina Rosicka
Faculty of Law, Institute of Economics I, ul. Straszewskiego 27, 31-113 Krakow
Tel: 221 033, ext. 406
Fax: 481 222 6306

*Programmes	-	In February 1992 the University began a 2-year postgraduate studies programme in Business and Market Economics.
	-	In October 1992 JU will start a full MBA programme.

*Funding and support	The programme of management education at the Jagiellonian University is mainly organized by the faculty of the University's Institute of Economics together with teachers from different European universities (within TEMPUS programmes: JEP 0578, coordinated by Economische Hogeschool, Limburg, Belgium; JEP 0982 coordinated by Oxford University) and a Consortium of Universities from the United States of America: University of Hartford, University of Massachussetts, Boston College and Columbia University.
	This cooperation has involved: the supply of books and teaching materials and equipment; the working together on the curriculum of business studies/ the training of the Polish faculty; Scholarships for Polish students, lecturers to business students given by teachers from the American and European universities.

SPAIN

Instituto de Estudios Superiores de la Empresa (IESE)

Prof. Victor Pou, Executive Manager IFDP
Avenida Pearson 21, 08034 Barcelona
Tel: (93) 204 4000 / 204 4100
Fax: (93) 280 11 77

*Experience The IESE of the University of Navarra, Barcelona, is one of the best business schools in Spain.

*Programmes IESE are taking part in a Joint European Project, together with SDA-Bocconi (Italy) and ISA-HEC (France), called the International Faculty Development Programme (IFDP). This programme is dedicated to the training of lectures of management from central and eastern European countries. The programme is starting at IESE in Barcelona, October 1992, and plans to annually train 100 central and eastern European professors of management and a total of 500 participants over the next five years. To carry out the IFDP, the IESE together with the two other founding western management schools have formed an Association to promote a European network of management training institutes in eastern Europe. For the full list of 14 eastern European institutions participating in this network see page section ...

*Funding The IESE along with the other founders of the IFDP is applying for grants to enable other eastern European schools to join the European network.

SWEDEN

Centrum för LedarUtveckling, Management Development Centre (CLU)

Director: Mr. Carl-Ivar Malm
CLU, Universitetet och Tekniska Högskolan i Linköping, S-581 83 Linköping
Tel: +46 132 824 45
Fax: +46 132 818 73

*Experience	CLU is an independent research unit within Linköping University.

*Programmes	CLU provides 2-week programmes for persons and organizations concerned with the development of small and medium-sized enterprises. One course was held in October 1991 for participants from the former Soviet Union, and another in December 1991 for participants from the Baltic states. A third course of the same kind is scheduled for participants from Russia in April 1992. The resource group are members of faculty who have extensive experience of East-Westjoint ventures. CLU is coordinator of an EC funded Comett project entitled SMED (small and Medium-sized Enterprise Development). One of the Faculty members is developing training programmes for the former GDR based on the SMED prototype.

SWITZERLAND

International Institute for Management Development (IMD)

In charge of East European Programme: Dr. Yury Boshyk
Chemin de Bellerive 23, P.O. Box 915, CH-1001 Lausanne
Tel: 4121 618 0111 or 618.03.18
Fax: 4121 266 725

*Experience	IMD is one of the leading business schools in the world, with extensive links back over 40 years. In this period its faculty have helped the countries of the region develop their own Education programmes and taught students from eastern Europe. IMD has also two eastern European Business Associates - Iskra and Prombudbank.

*Programmes	1. Visiting Fellows Programme. The purpose of this programme is:

- to provide the most advanced teachers of management and top managers from central and eastern Europe with a chance to participate on IMD programmes and to interact professionally with the IMD faculty. IMD's contribution would be to charge only 1/2 the usual fee.

- to provide intellectual and research guidance to international foundations or firms who wish to send funded and qualified personnel to work with IMD faculty on projects related to central and eastern Europe.

2. Special IMD Programmes and Workshops

The purpose is to provide an orientation to western firms on developments in central and eastern Europe. IMD has organized workshops for GE and for 50 executives and Government leaders invited by Hewlett-Packard.

3. Integration with IMD Teaching and Research Activities

The purpose of this activity is to include central and eastern Europe experiences in IMD programmes and research projects.

4. IMD, INSEAD, London Business School Consortium

The purpose of the consortium is:

-   to assist in the management education of central and eastern Europe by concentrating on educating the teachers of management, and future business leaders.

Training the trainer in the West comprises:

-   4 week academic programme and a 3 week "practicum" involving participating firms, with a one week "wrap-up";

-   held 3 times a year;

-   involving 40 participants each time: two group from central and eastern Europe, and one from the former Soviet Union alternating annually;

-   3 year project.

*Funding   The consortium programme is applying for funds from the EC, European Bank for Reconstruction and Development, participating firms and East European management institutes.

UNITED KINGDOM

Ashridge Management College (AMC)

Dean: Peter Beddowes
Berkhamsted, Hertfordshire HP4 1NS
Tel: (0442) 843 491 / 842 311
Fax: (0442) 842 382

*Experience	AMC was established in 1959.

*Experience   AMC was established in 1959.

*Programmes   Ahsridge has no plans for programmes specifically focused on East-West Joint ventures but organizes twice broad range of activities which are of relevance to the general area of East-West cooperation:

- a series of tailored programmes for Chief Executive Officers and Directors of Czechoslovakian enterprises. Ashridge designing and delivering management development programmes followed up with action planning/consulting support to be funded by the British Council starting in 1992. This initiative is designed to help 60 CEO's become more effective at leading their market economy enterprises. The programme will include visits to appropriate UK companies.

- European Management Programme. This is an open programme which is designed for managers who have to develop strategy and manage pan-European businesses. Ashridge runs this programme in conjunction with three other European Business Schools.

- East European Bursary scheme. Ashridge is able to provide financial assistance to a number of senior managers from eastern Europe to attend appropriate management development programmes at Ashridge. For further details contact Ashridge.

*Funding   Schemes are to be funded by the British Council.

....

University of Bradford Management Centre (UBMC)

Emm Lane, Bradford, West Yorkshire BD9 4JL
Tel: (0274) 542 299
Fax: (0274) 546 866

*Experience   The UBMC is currently involved in eastern Europe, particularly with the management of East-West joint ventures.

*Programmes   Current projects are:

- Management Link Project with the University of Miskolc, Hungary, and the establishment of a regional management centre for a train the trainer programme;

- Polish Academic Links Project with the Academy of Economics in Poznan, with modular training sessions on "management development in the new Europe";

- Potential projects include the Academy of Sciences in Prague and the Budapest University of Economics in Hungary, the project will include Trinity College in Dublin and Tilburg University in Netherlands.

....

Cranfield School of Management (CSM)

Cranfield, Bedford MK43 0AL
Tel: +44 234 751 122
Fax: +44 234 751 806

*Experience   The study of eastern European development is of significant interest to the
                school, and it has established a joint venture with Sofia International
                Management School in Hungary. The school was also originally involved in the
                IMC-Budapest.

*Programmes   Current activities include a general management programme for senior
                managers of the former USSR Radio; designing management programmes for
                SIMS in Bulgaria; having Bulgarian managers attending courses at the school;
                joint research projects with the Budapest University of Economic Sciences.

....

London Business School (LBS)

Sussex Place, Regent's Park, London NW1 4SA
Tel: +44 071 262 5050
Fax: +44 071 724 7875

*Experience   LBS belongs to the leading business schools of the world although its
                experience with eastern Europe management development dates only from
                1989.

*Programmes   The London Business School runs a series of three-week programmes for top
                managers from the former Soviet Republics.

                The programmes deal with management at the level of the individual
                enterprise. They focus on the experience of western managers in bringing
                about major changes in their own companies. Many of the issues these
                managers have faced correspond closely to questions now confronting managers
                in the Soviet Union. The programme's content is organized around these key
                issues:

                    ·   entering new markets
                    ·   product innovation
                    ·   internal restructuring in mature companies
                        -   entrepreneurship and incentives
                        -   flexible working practices and fair play
                        -   tracing productivity to its roots

- achieving and maintaining quality
- creating substitute employment
· composing the business plan for a new business
· constructing databases and information networks to support these activities.

50% of time is spent in visits to companies and in discussions with managers. 50% is spent in sessions with LBS faculty members, to establish frameworks for visits, obtain reference material and discuss questions raised by the visits.

80% of the managers attending these courses came from enterprises in high-technology sectors, and many of these enterprises have been actively negotiating with foreign partners to form joint ventures.

The first course took place in April 1989. The series was interrupted in mid-1991 and will be resumed in mid-1992.

....

Loughborough University Business School (LUBS)

Loughborough, Leicestershire, LE11 3TU
Tel: 0509 263 171
Fax: 0509 210 232

*Experience   Faculty members have specialized in trade-related issues in eastern Europe.

*Programmes   LUBS is currently at the stage of preliminary discussions with the Interindustrial Institute of Postgraduate Training for Managers at the Leningrad Institute of Engineering Economics. LUBS hope to develop training programmes for Soviet managers at Loughborough, and British managers in Leningrad.

*Funding   Sponsors are interested companies.

....

Manchester Business School (MBS)

Booth Street West, Manchester M15 6PB
Tel: 061 275 6333
Fax: 061 273 7732

*Experience   MBS, established in 1965, Under the University of Manchester, belongs to the more renowned business schools in Europe.

*Programmes   MBS has a USSR Senior Management Programme lasting 3 weeks and contains a 3-day internship. It focuses on the management of joint business activities between firms from the former Soviet Union and the UK. MBS collaborates with the Higher Commercial Management School in Moscow. MBS also runs short-term management courses, besides regular MBA programmes.

UNITED STATES OF AMERICA

Johnson Graduate School of Management (JGM)

Director of Executive Education: Dr. Graig M. McAllaster
Cornell University, Malott Hall, Ithaca, NY 14853-4201
Tel: 607 255 4251
Fax: 607 254 4590

*Experience	JGM at the Cornell University belongs to the so called Ivy League schools of the USA.
*Programmes	Together with SDA-Bocconi (Italy) and Lovanium International Management Centre (Belgium), JGM has designed an Advanced European Management Seminar programme. Two seminars given (in 1992) is specifically concerned about East and central European issues: "The new European economy" and "Business opportunities in eastern Europe". The seminars are primarily intended for western managers who want to gain an insight in the process of transition of the eastern economies, as well as doing business in the region.
*Funding	Seminar fees.

....

The Fuqua School of Business (FSB)

Duke University, Durham, NC 27706
Tel: (919) 660 6342
Fax: (919) 660 3607

*Experience	FSB, established in 1969, is recognized as being one of top ten American business schools.
*Programmes	Besides qualification programmes, such as the MBA, the FSB started a programme for Soviet management development in 1990. The programme contains a corporate internship, and a 3-week theory module. The training programme is offered twice a year to a group of 35-45 Soviet managers.
*Funding	The programme was initiated by a private donation. Financing for the student is done through his partner in a joint venture, the participating US firm sponsors the student during the internship period.

....

Harvard Graduate School of Business Administration (HBS)

Harvard University, Boston, MA 02163
Tel: 617 495 6161
Fax: 617 495 6999

*Experience   HBS is renowned for its MBA and Advanced Management Programmes, and is considered to be one of the worlds top-ten business schools.

*Programmes   Together with MIT, Wharton, Stanford and Northwestern, the HBS is undertaking a train the trainer programme which will begin in summer of 1992 (see p.28).

*Funding   First years class is being fully sponsored, for which 100-120 students are expected to enroll.

....

The International Institution of Entreprenology (IIE)

Washington DC Regional Office, P.O. Box 3609, Winchester, VA 22601
Fax: (703) 722 9522

*Programmes   The IIE will in 1992 run a series of "Growth Management" programmes for East European nations, which will include such features as new and redirected market; venture and growth capital; enterprise design; and creative adminstration. Length of the programme will be 2 1/2 days. Number of participants in each seminar will be 50, which are to be selected from top management in both the private and public sectors, specifically those with responsibilities for deciding on human resource training. Host nations for the initial series of programmes will be: Romania, Hungary, Czechoslovakia, Poland and Russia.

*Funding   The programme is joint sponsored by the IIE and the World Assembly of SME's.

....

MGL Corporation (MGL)

Suite 209, Two Neshaminy Interplex, Trevose, PA 1903
Tel: 215 244 4600
Fax: 215 244 4759

*Experience   MGL is a US-based company that has been providing products and services to government ministries and state-owned companies in the USSR and eastern Europe. It has also begun to assist US and other western businesses and individuals wishing to develop new markets in the region. It has branches in Moscow, Kemerovo and Vladivostok.

*Programmes	MGL's basic course provides a 3-week introduction, in the Russian language, to finance, marketing, accounting and organizational development. The programme can, if needed, be held in other East European languages as well. Training is conducted solely at the US facility while the USSR offices carry on consulting, trading and services. MGL is affiliated with the Moscow State Technical University. Course length are generally 2-6 weeks.

....

Katz Graduate School of Business (KGSB)

University of Pittsburgh, 372 Mervis Hall, Pittsburgh, PA 15260
Tel: (412) 648 1500
Fax: (412) 648 1693

*Programmes	KGSB is currently engaged in cooperative programmes with the International Management Centre in Budapest (Hungary) and the Czechoslovakian Management Centre in Prague. These are seminar series held 1991, over two days. Dealing specifically with the central European infrastructure, and the financing for the development of it.
*Funding	Privately sponsored and funded.

....

THUNDERBIRD, Department of International Studies

Director: Mr. William Kane
TMC-Thunderbird Management Center
American Graduate School of
 International Management
15249 N.59th Avenue
GLENDALE, Arizona 85306
USA
Tel: (602) 439-9622
Fax: (602) 978-7181

*Experience	School is considered as one of the US's top ten management institutions.
*Programmes	The academic (Master's degree) course work at the American Graduate School of International Management includes the following course designations of interest: East-West Trade, Counter-trade and Offset Barter, Privatization and Entrepreneurship (including Joint Ventures). These courses are a part of Thunderbird's regular academic programme and are offered three times a year.
	The Thunderbird Management Center (TMC) is the executive training centre which offers custom designed executive training running from three days to three months. They cover various aspects of international operations - marketing, finance, foreign area assessments, etc. Language training is also

provided by TMC, with particular emphasis on English as a second language for business. The Center has provided training for OSAIS - sponsored programmes fro executives from third world countries, Management training programmes for Russian executives are due to begin in 1992.

*Funding   Programmes are custom-designed to suit the needs of each client. Courses for the training of central and East European managers are available on demand including courses on East-West joint ventures.

....

4.5 TRAINING RECOMMENDATIONS

Western Governments

Recognizing the importance of management development in economic reforms and joint venture success, western governments have placed management training and development high on their list of priorities in their technical assistance programmes to economies in transition. However, some problems have emerged in channelling this assistance to achieve its stated objectives and these are listed below.

● **Focus on an academic and less on practical approach:** Management is not an academic discipline like philosophy, economics or mathematics. It is properly learned only through practical application and requires to be taught accordingly. It is argued that too many resources are being misdirected into developing MBA programmes in eastern Europe when shorter, more practical courses might be more useful during the transition period.

● **Too much lecturing without allowing sufficient practice:** Financial assistance might be usefully targeted on schemes providing eastern European managers practical experience of managing companies. The number of well established joint ventures now operating in eastern Europe makes it possible for these schemes to be held in the countries themselves.

● **Transfer of western materials without proper adaptation:** To transfer ideas and knowledge about management successfully, the distinctive management culture and specific conditions operating in the economies in transition must be taken into account.

● **Lack of a permanent foreign faculty in eastern Europe:** Western management experts often spend insufficient time in teaching assignments in eastern Europe. One of the reasons is that from a financial point of view teaching in eastern Europe for these experts is not attractive enough to give up their salaries in the West.

● **Lack of attention to developing local training capabilities:** Western funding for training eastern European managers has been distributed disproportionately to western management schools rather than to eastern European establishments to develop local trainers (all but 5 % of the EC's Tempus budget for training purposes in 1991-92 went back to western based places of learning). As a rule successful teaching occurs where the teacher and the student share the same cultural values, background and language. Benefits are derived more quickly if the trainer of managers has intimate knowledge of, or is a citizen of, the country where the managers are being taught. It is therefore important to emphasize the training of trainers and managers in eastern Europe.

● **Lack of jointly designed programmes (EE + W):** Although some progress has been made overall there is insufficient collaboration between East and West on developing curricula, teacher and student exchanges, setting of internationally recognized qualifications and certificates and joint research and preparation of East European "case-studies" as teaching tools.

● **Insufficient attention being given to training managers in the industrial regions:** Western assistance in finance and expertise has been excessivley concentrated in the capitals, while much more attention should be paid to distributing this support to the regions. Currently in some eastern European capitals there are too many western consultants and trainers.

Bearing these problems in mind, western governments might usefully consider the following guidelines outlined in Box 8 for the future disbursal of funds to eastern Europe.

BOX 8

SUGGESTIONS FOR FUTURE STRATEGIES OF FOREIGN ASSISTANCE IN MANAGEMENT DEVELOPMENT

- Building up Local Management Development Capacities
- Concentrating on Training Managers in Recipient Countries
- Developing Joint Training Methodologies, Programme, Materials
- Mixed (western and eastern managers) Training Programme
- Emphasis on short-term, Pragmatic Management Training (basic management (MBA-type) education - later on)
- Focusing on Language Teaching
- More Attention to Entrepreneurship Training (owners - managers)
- Spreading efforts from Capitals to Industrial Centres and Regions
- Promoting "Training the Trainer" Programmes on the Basis of Long-Term and Close-Working Inter Institutional Relationships

---

Western companies

Western companies are confronted immediately with a number of dilemmas regarding the management of their businesses in eastern Europe: who to appoint as general manager ?; should they keep the existing management when buying companies in eastern Europe ?; how much control should be given to the east European affiliate, and so on.

Clearly the specific nature of each enterprise and its particular strategy and business objectives make any generalizations difficult. Nevertheless, based on the experience to date the following practical recommendations can be offered as guidelines for managers responsible for making the eastern European side of their company's businesses operational.

Local managers or western managers ? The first dilemma is whether to employ a local or a western manager to run the company ? Up till now, western companies have preferred to appoint western managers to senior posts within the company. As seen in the case of the Italian company, AGV, in Belarus, (see Case-Study No.2, page 33) the Italians gained a majority share of the joint venture in order to remove the local manager from the top post in the joint venture and to appoint an Italian CEO in his place. In this case as in others, the logic of the western partner has been clear: local managers do not know enough about western concepts of production, marketing and finance and are not accustomed to taking charge of businesses. While generally western companies express a commitment in the long term to appoint local managers to the top posts, in the short term they only trust responsibility to their own western managers.

Such a policy is however not without its drawbacks. First, there are few grounds for demonstrating that western managers are any more successful than local managers in running East-West joint ventures. Western managers are after all operating in alien environments. The economies of central and eastern Europe are nascent market economies; they do not as yet exhibit the business practices with which western trained business executives are familiar. Second, western managers command extremely high salaries and perks which are a source of resentment by local management. In Belarus as we noted a gap developed between "them" i.e. the local managers and "us", i.e., the western recruited executives, that destroyed any possibility of creating a team spirit.

Under these circumstances western companies may in fact be better served if they appoint local managers to head their eastern European operations. First of all, there is no substitute to a local manager when it comes to requiring information on indigenous markets and suppliers, networks and ministries, regulations and work-force strengths and weaknesses. A local manager is better equipped to look at possible partners and assess the worth of their experience, personnel, sources of supply, equipment, land and buildings. The right general manager is also a great help in negotiating an equitable business deal. It is true to say that eastern managers were never efficient in the western sense of the term but they gained a sort of excellence in coping with the perennial shortages and lack of infrastructure which still bedevil businesses in the East. Secondly, there is growing evidence that one of the main barriers to putting local managers in charge - their reluctance to take responsibility - can be overcome if their own financial performance is directly linked to the health of their company. Whether in Poland or Russia, ownership has the same effect as anywhere else - it encourages responsibility, adaptability and hard work. Devolving responsibility to local managers has, it appears, paid off for many joint ventures in Russia (see Case-Study No. 3, page 36).

Finding the right local managers. In the West searching for suitable business executives is facilitated by a number of factors: the procedures for announcing job openings, the newspapers and magazines which carry the adverts, the business schools which produce appropriate candidates are familiar to candidates and companies alike; second, background and references are easily checked and corroborated; third, business and general education attainments are widely understood, objective indications of a candidate's worth.

None of these factors necessarily applies in eastern European countries. Personal and professional history is often clouded in obscurity or compromised by politics. A candidate's knowledge of business is likely to be limited and is almost bound to be coloured by the misrepresentations of a communist education. The question of how and where to recruit the best local managers perplexes even the largest personnel departments of western firms.

Conventional wisdom in the West has held that since strong personal and hierarchical relationships governed the conduct of the communist economy, it is critical to hire a person firmly tied into the old networks. But now it is no longer sufficient to select managers with "good connections". The old networks have collapsed in central European countries and with the demise of many industry ministries in Russia and the other Republics of the CIS, such a policy has no longer much value.

A search for managerial talent in the economies in transition thus must focus less on industry relationships and connections but more on personal business experience, intelligence and integrity. The first joint ventures were formed almost five years ago in the economies in transition and many local managers recruited at this time will have gained invaluable experience that the second wave of foreign investors can put to good use. The new business schools also will be a useful starting point in the search for suitable managerial material (see pages 41-47). New local business papers and magazines where job advertisements can be placed are widely read and firms can expect hundreds of replies.

Once the initial selection is made, a rather long process takes place where candidates are brought to the headquarters of the company for extensive formal and informal interviewing. In many instances the line managers and the recruitment officers responsible for eastern Europe will have to devote considerable time in the selection procedure.

Training. In the start-up phase it is recommended that western companies train the managers themselves in the task they will perform in their home country. This will generally involve bringing the eastern European manager to a western based company to learn under the direct supervision of their western counterparts or the sending of the latter to the East. This training can be expected to take from between three months to one year and will take place before the company begins operations.

Selecting managers for training. Western companies should endeavour to ensure that they themselves are responsible for the selection of managers for training. In some early joint ventures the western partner was given all the local managers to train. It had no flexibility in hiring and firing or in selecting the most appropriate for training. In many cases after considerable sums had been spent it became clear that these managers - usually older and more senior - could not be retrained. Thus experience show that western firms will get best results if they pick younger managers who are flexible, enthusiastic and better prepared to accept new ideas.

Where eastern European managers can be best trained. As has been mentioned, it is no longer necessary to consider training managers only in the West. Eastern Europe now has developed a number of training establishments of high quality. Western companies can avoid the cost of sending their managers back home for training. Currently, the cost of training a manager for three months in Moscow is in the region of 10-20,000 roubles or USD 40-80. Sending 10 managers on such a course would cost a firm the same price as a return airline ticket to Moscow from any European destination. Local training provides western firms with other advantages: it gives a positive image of investing in local employees and shows commitment to the local economy. Finally the training should be built around actual local conditions and dealing with particular enterprise problems.

Choosing the right training establishments. If choosing an institution in eastern Europe to send its managers, a western firm should make its selection on the following basis:

- Has the establishment a well-trained faculty ?
- Has it close links with a western business school ? and
- Has it close connections with and recognized by local or foreign business ?

Participating in the new schools. It is recommended that western firms should take a closer look at local training establishments not just for training purposes but also for recruiting managers for their local business operations. Western firms might usefully contribute to the development of these new business institutions. It is in their interests after all that they develop them into effective business schools. Such involvement might take the form of being represented in the school's Board of Governors, providing teaching and internships to students, helping in the design of courses and syllabi, and assisting in funding.

5. MAJOR FINANCIAL SOURCES FOR EASTERN EUROPEAN MANAGEMENT DEVELOPMENT

In July 1989 the Group of Seven most industrialised countries (G-7) launched a programme in support of the economic reforms in Poland and Hungary and asked the European Commission to coordinate western assistance to these countries. The Group has since grown to include 24 countries (i.e. the 12 EC Member States, the 6 EFTA countries, Turkey, the USA, Canada, Japan, Australia and New Zealand) and is now known as the G-24 Group; meanwhile, assistance has been extended to include Bulgaria, former Czechoslovakia, Romania, Albania, Estonia, Latvia, Lithuania and parts of former Yugoslavia.

The G-24 Group does not itself finance or administer western assistance but acts as a forum, where western countries inform each other of their respective assistance efforts. Its activities are coordinated by the European Commission in order to reach a common approach in the assistance to the reforming countries, and to avoid overlapping and reach a synergy effect between the various multilateral and bilateral efforts. G-24 countries provide multilateral assistance, through varied channels such as the so-called Bretton Woods institutions (World Bank and IMF), the OECD or the newly created European Bank for Reconstruction and Development (EBRD), as well as important bilateral assistance.

Meanwhile, the European Community has also established its own programme to help central and East European countries (the EC's own PHARE programme). This programme is funded by the European Community budget and managed by the European Commission. It therefore comes in addition to individual EC countries' participation in bilateral and multilateral assistance schemes (World Bank, IMF, EBRD, etc.).

In the delivery of this aid, the private sector has been assigned a key role by the newly elected eastern authorities and western donor governments, as is reflected in the focus of the Group of 24 countries programmes and the philosophy of the EBRD. Finance varies from assistance for the setting-up of joint ventures, infrastructure projects, support for medium and small enterprises, and venture capital for start-up companies. Technical Assistance is also funded, particularly for training in the areas of macro- and micro- economic management techniques in order to facilitate the creation of a free-market system.

The volume of funds available for business and training are small in relation to financial lending to assist the balance of payments and currency stabilization and humanitarian aid. Direct financial assistance is provided both multilaterally by international financial institutions and by national governments. The following is a description of these agencies activities and the assistance which is currently being provided for training by governments.

1. *The European Bank for Reconstruction and Development*

The EBRD is a hybrid development and merchant bank that loans and invests only in the central and East European region for the express purpose of promoting the transition to market economies. The bank's mandate allows it to provide no less than 60% of its funds to the private sector, defined as private sector enterprises of"state-owned enterprises implementing a programme to achieve private ownership and control". This bank is also committed to improving the environment and projects which its supports must meet strict environmental criteria. Funds are to be provided on a commercial basis according to "sound banking and investment principles" and within commercial decision-making time frames.

The bank's stated objectives for funding projects are to: develop the private sector, implement privatization of state-owned enterprises, encourage direct foreign investment, reform and strengthen the financial sector, restructure the industrial sector, modernize infrastructure for private sector development, promote small and medium-sized enterprises and improve the environment.

The bank will make loans in convertible currency of ECU 5 million (USD 6.2 million) or more, take an equity stake of up to 15% and in some cases provide guarantees. In no cases will it take more than 35% of a particular deal. The bank's aim is to supplement private-sector financing, not to replace it. Proposals for both public sector infrastructure (physical and financial) and private sector projects of privatization will be considered if they meet the criteria above and have a credible business plan, a completed feasibility study, a strong sponsor(s) willing to make a significant capital commitment. Such projects should be suitable for funding in convertible currency and, most importantly, should be financially viable.

This Bank has two departments - development banking and merchant banking. The development banking department provides assistance for infrastructure projects and participates in co-financing projects. In the merchant banking department, financing is available for private sector or privatization-related projects. The EBRD along with the International Finance Corporation (IFC) (see page 95) has been increasing its equity investments in East European enterprises. Their participation has been welcomed by foreign investors at a time of high uncertainty. So far their equity investments have been concentrated in Hungary and the Czech and Slovak Republics. Towards the end of 1991 the EBRD made an equity investment in Ceskeslovenske Aerolinie, the state airline in partnership with Air France, and in Cokoladovn, the country's largest chocolate and biscuit producer. In the latter, Nestlé and BSN formed a joint venture which purchased 43 per cent of the capital of Cokoladovny. The EBRD's own share was 15 per cent and another 3.5 per cent has been purchased by a Czech financial investor, Investicni Banka. The Czech and Slovak Republics will provisionally hold 34 per cent until the shares are listed on the stock exchange, while the national restitution fund will hold 4.5 per cent of the capital.

The average size of the investments so far undertaken has been (USD 25.8 million). In its first year of operations the Bank has injected more than USD 2 billion into the economies of eastern Europe.

Since the Bank's inauguration more countries have become members: Albania, Estonia, Latvia and Lithuania and the republics of the former Soviet Union, except Georgia.

Proposals for private sector or privatization related projects should be submitted to: Ronald Freeman, first Vice-president, Merchant Banking, European Bank for Reconstruction and Development, 122 Leadenhall St, London EC3V 4EB, Tel: (071) 3386 000.

Proposals for physical and financial infrastructure projects should be submitted to : Mario Sarcinelli, Vice-President, Development Banking, European Bank for Reconstruction and Development (address as above).

2. The European Economic Community

(i) The PHARE Programme

Initially set up for Poland and Hungary, the Community's PHARE programme was subsequently extended to include the former Czechoslovakia, Bulgaria, former Yugoslavia (currently on hold), Romania, Albania and the Baltic States. The former Soviet Union gets a separate technical assistance fund. It is financed from funds, specifically made available for this purpose in the annual Community budget. These funds are made available as non-reimbursable grants to finance projects and reconstruction programmes and not in the form of loans for commercial activities. PHARE's aid must be used primarily to support the process of reform in the beneficiary countries, in particular by financing or participating in the financing of projects aimed at economic restructuring in certain priority areas: agriculture, industry, investment, energy, training, environmental protection, trade and services.

In practice, this implies the transformation of the production and distribution systems with an emphasis on private ownership and investment as well as the establishment of the broader regulatory, organized and commercial infrastructure and environment without which a competitive market economy can neither function properly nor attract investment.

Thus, the core areas of this process, closely interlinked and directly related to the establishment of a market system are:

- abolition of State monopolies;
- restructuring and privatisation of public enterprises;
- modernisation of financial services;
- promotion of the private sector, particularly small-and medium sized enterprises;
- development of the labour market and social sector including the reform of social security and welfare policies.

It is clearly the responsibility of the governments of the recipient countries to define the respective policies, priorities, sequence and timing of the restructuring of their economies. It is for them to decide for what particular purposes and measures PHARE aid should be used.

The Commission responds to the recipient countries' requests providing financial support, supplies, technical assistance, training and studies for particular programmes of reform in key sectors as appropriate.

It follows therefore that PHARE programmes have to be initiated by the respective national authorities and presented to the Commission through the designated official coordinators. Preference is given to sectoral development programmes to support policy reforms rather than to one-off individual projects. Any ideas for programmes and projects should therefore be submitted not to the Commission but to the appropriate interlocutors or governmental authorities in the recipient countries. If such proposals are accepted by the recipient countries as part of a wider reconstruction programme, they may be presented to the Commission for financing.

(ii) Trans-European Mobility Programme for University Studies (TEMPUS)

TEMPUS has the prime objective of promoting the development of higher education systems in the PHARE beneficiary countries, particularly by means of student mobility.

Financial support under the TEMPUS SCHEME falls into two main categories:

- *Joint European Projects* (JEPs). Grants of up to ECU 500,000 per year are payable to consortia comprising at least one organization from a PHARE country and organizations from at least two EEC States. Almost 500 JEPs have already been established.

- *Mobility Grants*. These are available to students, and to teaching and administrative staff, for periods of up to a year. Travel may be in either direction although the principal beneficiary should be in the East. Over 7000 students and teachers have been supported in this way.

There is a broad list of eligible sectors including the physical, life and social sciences. For additional information contact: EC TEMPUS Office, 45 Rue de Trèves, B-1040 Brussels; Tel: (322) 238 7833; Fax: (322) 238 7733.

(iii) Joint-Venture PHARE Programme (JOPP)

This scheme, which is part of the overall PHARE Programme, has the aim of encouraging private sector investment in central and eastern Europe by means of joint ventures between EC-based businesses and local partners. It consists of four facilities designed to cover the whole process of joint venture investment:

- *Facility 1: Identification of possible projects and potential partners.* To provide assistance in the exploration of business opportunities through general actions not linked to individual investment projects.

- *Facility 2: Preliminaries to establishing a Joint Venture.* This covers part of the costs of undertaking feasibility studies, market analysis and contract negotiations between the partners. Seed money for early-stage investments would also be included. EC support is in the form of an interest-free advance covering half of the eligible costs up to a maximum of ECU 75,000. If a joint venture is actually set up, the other half of the project costs would be advanced.

- *Facility 3: Capital Requirements.* The EC may contribute to the capital financing requirements and take on part of the risks on equitable terms with other investors. The contribution is limited to 20% of the total capital needs of the joint venture up to a maximum of ECU 1 m. This must be paid within 10 years.

- *Facility 4: Technical Assistance.* This is to strengthen the human resources development of the joint ventures by co-financing specific technical assistance measures and transfer of know-how. Financial support is in the form of an interest-free loan covering up to 50% of the eligible costs up to a maximum of ECU 150,000.

The scheme is based on a network of financial intermediaries selected by the Commission throughout the Member States. The role of this network is to promote the scheme, to identify potential investors, to assess the projects which are submitted, to arrange co-financing if necessary, to administer the funds allocated to the beneficiaries on behalf of the Commission and to follow up the projects which are approved by the Commission. Priority is given to small and medium-sized enterprises (SMEs) and to joint ventures with net fixed assets below 10 m ECE. To obtain additional information contact: M. Tarillon, Commission of the European Communities, Head of Unit, Wagner Building, L-2920 Luxembourg; Tel: 43 63 50; Fax: 43 63 22.

(iv) Technical Assistance to the Confederation of Independent States and Georgia (TACIS)

Under the TACIS Programme the EC has allotted ECU 850 m over two years to support development projects throughout the 12 states.

It functions in a similar manner to the PHARE Programme: The five priority areas are:

- human resources development;
- food production and distribution;
- networks: energy, transport, telecommunications;
- enterprise support services;
- nuclear safety.

In contrast to the PHARE programme however, capital projects are not supported. Most of the funding is for the provision of policy advice, institutional reform and the creation of legal and regulatory frameworks. Equipment crucial to these measures may also be financed.

Although the funds are made directly available to state or local governments, co-operatives, or to state or private enterprises, TACIS does offer opportunities for consultants. Potential applicants should contact the Commission Director General I (DGI) to be included in the Central Consultancy Register. To obtain additional information contact: Mr. Joannes Ter Haar, Commission of the European Communities, DGI-E-2 TACIS, 200 rue de la Loi, B-1049 Brussels; Tel: (322) 235 3544; Fax: (322) 296 6012.

(v) Action for Cooperation in the Field of Economics (ACE)

ACE also forms part to the PHARE programme and is aimed at stimulating the exchange of economic research activities and viewpoints between the Community and beneficiary countries. The future of this programme is currently under review.

Support is given, in whole or in part, to the financing of:

- scholarships and research grants to enable eastern European economists, including doctoral students and post-doctoral researchers, to spend time at a higher education establishment or research institute in the Community;

- high level seminars for economists and senior civil servants of the PHARE beneficiary countries;

- multi-national networks or research projects including at least one eastern European and two Community higher education or research institutes;

- active participation of eastern European economists at conferences;

- recognized eastern European establishments offering international PhDs in economic science and MBA courses.

For additional information contact: Mr. D. Descoutures, Commission of the European Communities, Directorate XII-H-1-ACE, 200 rue de la Loi, B-1049 Brussels; Tel: (322) 235 6876; Fax: (322) 236 3307.

3. *The European Investment Bank*

The European Investment Bank (EIB), which is owned by the EC Member States who all subscribe to its capital, finances capital investment projects to promote the balanced development of the Community. It operates as a bank, raising the bulk of its financial resources on capital markets to fund projects meeting Community priority objectives. Awarded a first class "AAA" credit rating, the Bank on-lends the proceeds of its borrowing to finance projects on a non-profit basis at cost plus 0.15% to cover administrative expenses. The EIB is financially independent and is not funded by the Community budget. EIB support is provided following invitations from the Council of the EC to the Bank to participate, within the framework of a Community programme. As part of the Community's cooperation policy with central and eastern European countries, the EIB finances projects in Bulgaria, Czech and Slovak Republics, Hungary, Poland and Romania; in addition it has operated in the former Yugoslavia for many years.

In these countries, the EIB grants loans to viable public and private sector projects in infrastructure, industry, agro-industry, agriculture, energy, tourism and services of benefit to these sectors. It supports capital investment in priority sectors and gives particular emphasis to infrastructure projects which play key roles in the new orientation to encourage exports and to restructure the industrial sector, e.g. energy, telecommunications and transport, the environment and industrial projects, especially those involving joint-ventures with EC enterprises. The EIB carries out appraisals of the economic, technical and financial viability of each project it finances and ensures the investment is in keeping with a country's commitments undertaken towards the international institutions within the framework of the restructuring of national economies. The agreement of the authorities concerned is necessary. The EIB can provide loans up to 50% of the cost of a project. It can co-finance investment with other project financing institutions.

For larger scale projects, the EIB makes available individual loans either directly to a project promoter, or indirectly through a government or banking intermediary. The State and private or public companies, with or without the participation of foreign investors, have access to EIB finance on equal terms. Small and medium sized projects with a total investment cost below ECU 15-20 million are financed through global loans. These are similar to temporary lines of credit opened with banks or financial intermediaries operating on a national or regional basis, which then use the proceeds to fund projects selected on the basis of the criteria of the EIB.

The EIB was invited in 1989 by the Council to grant loans of up to ECU 1 billion for both Poland and Hungary. In May 1991, it was invited to grant loans of up to ECU 700 million to cover funding of projects in Bulgaria, former Czechoslovakia, and Romania on the same terms. The EIB's initial lending in Poland, Hungary and Romania focused on the energy, telecommunications and transport sectors. Global loans were also granted to two banks in Poland and Hungary.

European Investment Bank
100 Boulevard Konrad Adenauer
L-2950 Luxembourg
Tel: 352 43791
Fax: 352 437704

4. The World Bank

The World Bank is constituted by four closely associated institutions:

- the international Bank for Reconstruction and Development (IBRD), which lends funds to those creditworthy developing countries with relatively high per capita income. The interest rate is variable, set at 0.5% above the Banks's average cost of borrowing. The Bank only provides loans to governments or loans guaranteed by governments.

- the international Finance Corporation (IFC), which provides loans and risk capital to finance private projects in developing countries, in collaboration with other investors as well as financial, legal and technical advice to private enterprises. It does not require government guarantees of repayment. To date it has been the most important single source of private financing in central and eastern Europe, mostly through co-financing projects with the EIB;

- the international Development Association (IDA) which provides assistance to the poorest developing countries on concessional terms;

- the Multilateral Investment Guarantee Agency (MIGA) which provides investors with insurance against non-commercial risks: It also provides advisory services on means to improve the country's environment for foreign investment.

Hungary, Poland, former Czechoslovakia, Bulgaria, Romania and Albania have all joined the World Bank.

The bank has allocated USD 9 billion for development projects in Eastern Europe for 1991-1993. Priority areas include privatisation, infrastructure modernisation, the rehabilitation of the environment, the development of a market system and the reorganization of the social welfare system. Only governments can propose projects for financial assistance. The borrower is then responsible for all procurement associated with Bank-financed projects, related to goods, equipment and services.

World Bank   Headquarters: 1818 H Street, N.W., Washington, D.C. 20433, USA
    Tel: (202) 477-1234
    Fax: (202) 477-6391

    European office: 66, Avenue d'Iena, 75116 Paris, France
    Tel: (1) 40 69 30 00
    Fax:(1) 47 20 19 66

5. The International Monetary Fund (IMF)

The International Monetary Fund (IMF) provides policy advice to governments, balance of payments financing as well as technical assistance in a number of areas ranging from helping to establish a central bank to the development of financial markets. IMF financial assistance aims to help countries meet temporary payment needs. The CIS, Poland, Hungary, Czechoslovakia, Bulgaria, Romania and Albania are all members of the IMF. In 1991 alone, the IMF lent around USD 3.6 billion to eastern Europe.

6. The Inter Europa Bank

This is Hungary's fully diversified, wholesale, commercial bank now providing services to corporations. It was involved in the country's first privatization programme.

7. Danish Investment Fund

To qualify for this Danish venture capital fund, applicants need to have a valid business plan and the idea must contribute to the social and economic development of the host country. There is a ceiling of USD 3 million a project, and the fund keeps up to 40% of the total finance required for the business. The fund also takes 30% of the share capital and is willing to finance 25% of the total financial requirement of a project. In 1990, the fund awarded DKK 150 million. Seven joint ventures were signed up in that year, five in Poland, one in Hungary and one in former Czechoslovakia.

The scheme considers all strata - from small cooperatives to large state-owned banks. In some cases it might be training high-level managers or government officials.

5.2 GOVERNMENTS

1. Austria

The Austrian Government has created a special "Projekt Management- und Berufsausbildung" (Professional and Management Training Project) for eastern Europe and has produced a set of guidelines for disbursing financial assistance for management training. Its financial assistance for training is targeted at: young managers training for middle and upper management; government officials and interest-groups, skilled workers, apprentices and trainers.

Training eligible for assistance should in principle be in the respective partner's own country unless the joint venture is involved in tourism or in another activity where a visit to the Austrian company would be beneficial.

Costs Covered under the Project

BMfwA: Costs incurred by the lecturer: fee; preparation of documentation and material; travel.

Austrian partner: as a single cost (at least 25% of the total cost): organization in Austria; possible costs of stay of the participant in Austria.

Foreign Partner: Infrastructure costs in the country for example: renting of seminar rooms; Hiring of lecturers; participants' costs.

Further conditions:

- Applications are made by the Austrian side, in consultation with the foreign partner.
- The lecturer/Trainer should be Austrian.

- Foreign Institutes must be in the position to make their own financial contributions and be able to explain their aims to the targets Group.
- In other respects, the general guiding principle of management applies to the grant for assistance from the funds of the Federation.

During 1991, the Austrian Federal Economic Chamber has held altogether 195 seminars in Poland, former Czech and Slovak Federal Republics, Hungary, Bulgaria, Romania, Ukraine, Slovenia and Mongolia for top and middle management who wanted to learn more about western-type management, marketing, financing, personnel management, etc. The duration of the seminars were from 3 days to several weeks. In the course of 1992 the Austrian Federal Economic Chamber provided special programmes for managers of joint ventures in the former Czech and Slovak Federal Republics and Hungary.

For further details contact either Dr Peter Kowar or Dr Horst Machu, Austrian Federal Economic Chamber, Wiedner Hauptstraße 63, 1045 Vienna, Austria.

2. *Belgium*

Belgium has allocated a BEF 630 million budget as bilateral aid to East and central Europe. Within this bilateral budget, BEF 120 million are earmarked for the support of the Société Belge d'Investissement International (SBI) which helps Belgian SMEs investing in East Europe (except Albania) and BEF 120 million are directed to the training in Belgium of future East European managers. Moreover the Office National du Ducroire, which aims to stimulate Belgian external trade, mainly by insuring against export credit risk, has created new facilities for guarantees of operations with East Europe (export and investment).

Société Belge d'Investissement
International
63 rue Montoyer, 1040 Brussels.
Tel: 02/230 27 85
Fax: 02/231 13 31

Office National du Ducroireé
40 Square de Meeûs, 1040 Brussels
Tel: 02/509 42 11
Fax: 02/513 50 59

3. *Canada*

The Central and East European Task Force, set up within the Ministry of Foreign Affairs and International Trade, coordinates Canada's bilateral assistance to central and eastern Europe. This assistance takes the form of humanitarian and food aid, technical assistance, export credit financing and training.

In addition a programme called Renaissance helps Canadian companies to set up joint ventures in eastern Europe, and provides training courses in management and technical areas.

Mr. Redjon
Central and Eastern European Task Force
Ministry of Foreign Affairs and International Trade
125 Promenade Sussex, Ottawa, Ontario, K1N8L5
Tel: 1. 613992 20 98

4. Denmark

Danish bilateral assistance is mainly directed toward Poland, Hungary, Czech and Slovak Republics, and the Baltic Republics. The Danish government has launched several initiatives to help East European companies and to help Danish companies to invest in eastern Europe. The main initiatives are the following:

- An Investment Fund for Central and Eastern Europe (the IO Fonden) provides financing for joint ventures.

> IO-Fonden
> Bremerholm 4, 1069 Copenhagen K.
> Tel: 45.33 14 25 75

- Management training courses are provided by the Ministry of Industry for East European managers.

> Industri og-Handelsstyrelsen
> Industri Ministeriet
> Tagensvej 137, 2200 Copenhagen N
> Tel: 45.31 85 10 66
> Fax: 45.31 81 70 68

- An Environmental Support Scheme gives assistance to environmental projects.

> National Agency for Environmental Protection
> Strandgade 29
> DK-1401 Copenhagen K
> Tel: 45.31 57 83 10
> Fax: 45.31 57 24 49

- A Fund managed by the Ministry of Foreign Affairs provides grants to projects related to eastern Europe.

> Udenrigsministeriet (Min. of Foreign Affairs)
> Asiatisk Plads 2, 1148 Copenhagen K
> Tel: 45.33.92 00
> Fax: 45.31 54 05 33

5 Finland

The Ministry of Trade and Industry organizes management courses (a FIM 2.5 million budget has been allocated for 1992). Training courses are also organized by other Ministries (Finance, Education) as well as by the Central Bank. Training courses in the food industry are also given. For further information contact:

Mr. Suikkanen
Ministry of Foreign Affairs
External Trade Dept.
Tel: 358.0.134 15627

Finnish Export Credit Limited
Eteläesplanadi 8
SF 00130 Helsinki
Tel: 358.0. 131 171
Fax: 358.0. 174 819

6. *France*

In the context of its programme of bilateral cooperation with the countries of eastern Europe, the French Minister of Foreign Affairs has undertaken a number of different projects on management training. The most important have been to establish in certain of these countries, permanent training structures, generally jointly financed and jointly managed between France and the host-country. Those establishments of this kind and which are currently operational are:

- L'Institut Franco-Tchécoslovaque de Gestion (IFTG) de Prague;

- Le Centre Franco-Bulgare de Formation à la Gestion (MARCOM) de Sofia;

- Le Centre Français de Formation et d'Information des Cadres (CEFFIC) de Varsovie (training in management and insurance);

- Le Centre Franco-Polonais de Formation Bancaire de Katowice (which will soon establish an affiliate in Warsaw);

- Le Centre Paris-Moscou Business de Moscou (Partenariat CEGOS-Ecole Supérieure de Commerce de Moscou);

- Le Partenariat Chambre de Commerce et d'Industrie de Paris-Académie du Commerce Extérieur de Moscou, which offers a Masters in Management;

- Le Centre de Formation Bancaire du Centre International de Formation aux Professions Bancaires (CIFPB) de Moscou;

- Le Partenariat ESIDEC de Metz-Institut des Finances et de l'Economie de St-Petersbourg.

In parallel to these activities, the French Government also provides financial support to a great number of specific projects on management training in a number of different areas: enterprise management, management in banking, administration management in local councils, etc. These activities cover the whole of central and eastern Europe, under various forms: apprenticeships in French establishments, training seminars and training missions to the countries concerned.

Czech and Slovak Republics

In the Czech and Slovak Republics training of managers is coordinated by the *Institut Franco-Tchécoslovaque de Gestion* (IFTG) under the direction of the French Embassy's Cultural and Scientific Service.

The IFTG (Stepanska 18, 11000 Prague, Tel: 42.2.22.58.06, Fax: 42.2.26.67.07) offers two types of training:

- Longer term training programmes in French to French-speaking managers. Those programmes are based on training modules in managements (markets economy, marketing, information technology, production management, financial management) and on training placements or apprenticeships with French companies.

- Teachers from French schools of Business and Management Training Institutes also offer courses with the assistance of Czech teachers who have been trained in France.

The purpose of these jointly provided courses, the training of trainers and the joint publication of research is to foster on the one hand, the creation of a stable corps of trainers in the country and on the other, to create links between French and Czech and Slovak institutions.

The Association called *"Gestionnaires sans Frontières"*:

- The *"Gestionnaires sans Frontières"* Association covers training based on practical exchanges between enterprises, encouraging two-way contacts between enterprises. This training is entrusted to enterprise professionals and school professors. It is given in the form of workshops.

- "L'école nationale des Ponts et Chaussées" through its MIB programme develops an English MBA programme in cooperation with l'Ecole Supérieure Technique de Prague (CVU). Management lectures are given by ENPC Group Professors. The programme aims at training enterprise managers through practical placements.

- The French Government also helps in the training of prospective enterprise managers. Thus some scholarships are granted to Czech and Slovak students enabling them to stay in France for a year in commerce schools or specialised programmes of training in management for central and eastern European students (for example COPERNIC Programme within ENPC).

Hungary

The French Government has supported since its founding in Budapest, the Centre for the Training of Banking Personnel. This Centre was created by the Centre Français de Formation Bancaire (CFFB).

Poland

The French programme of Technical and Training Assistance was launched towards the end of 1989. It is based on the France-Poland Foundation (Foundation France-Pologne (EFP)) and on the central and eastern European interministerial Mission (Mission Interministérielle pour l'Europe Centrale et Orientale (MIECO)), entrusted with the coordinating of French assistance to this region. Support comes from the FFP and the Ministry of Foreign Affairs, and additional co-financing, community credits, and funds from local organizations.

Projects are selected in consultation with the Polish authorities (plenipotentiary for the cooperation abroad, Mr. Sariusz-WolskI). Financial support is directed at achieving two goals: the strengthening of a state of law and assistance in the transition to a market economy.

Under its Enterprise management *programme the most important projects are:*

- the programme of the *Institut Français de Gestion* ((IFG) Management French Institute) brought into operation within CEFFIC: 750 apprentices over a period of 3 years for 2-week apprenticeships with a great utilization of computer instruments.
To this basic programme more specialized information can be added such as human resources management, management audit, finance analyses (400 apprentices are expected for 1992).

- Cooperation between INSEP and the Academy of Economics of Szcecin: around 200 apprentices for 1991.

- Cooperation between the School of International Commerce of Rynia and several high-levelled French schools such as INSEP, EDHEC and EAP.

- Opening, in October 1991, and the Ecole Supérieure of Katowice, in cooperation with the Ecole Supérieure de Commerce de Toulouse. Project co-financed by the EEC (TEMPUS programme). Training covers a period of 3 years for approximately 30 students a year.

- Creation of a Masters in industrial management in the Polytechnic of Wmoclaw, Poland.

- *CEFFIC (Centre Français de Formation et d'Information des Cadres)*

Since the end of 1990, an important part of its training programmes was established in Warsaw, under the auspices of CEFFIC. The French Government has entirely renovated a building in the rue Senatorska, to assist in management training. From January to October 1991, 850 apprentices have followed training courses (namely IFG, CNFPT, Chambers of Commerce), the workshops and conferences. In 1992, around 2500 apprentices will follow courses organized by this establishment.

7. *Germany*

There is no direct financial assistance to German firms wishing to invest or set up joint ventures in eastern Europe. The Federal government provides advice and organizes management training courses for eastern Europeans and for German firms wishing to set up their own programmes and some Länder have set up investment guarantee funds to promote investment in certain eastern European countries.

Firms interested in doing business or investing in eastern Europe must contact the relevant Ministries depending on the area of business in which they are involved.

Germany has been the most generous of all the western governments in granting direct, government-to-government aid to central and eastern Europe. General information about German involvement in such assistance should be obtained from:

Mr. Dalhof
Auswertigesamt (Ministry of Foreign Affairs)
Adenauer Allé 99 - 103, 5300 Bonn 1 (Postfach 1148)
Tel: 49.228.171

8. *Italy*

On 26 February 1992, the Italian Parliament approved a Law No.212 to provide financial assistance for training and technical assistance for personnel of joint-venture with Italian enterprises established in central and eastern Europe. The main purpose of the law is to support the transition process in these countries. In this connection Law No.212 provides for financial support related to "economic, social, scientific, technological, formative and cultural cooperation" with these countries. Article 3 of the law envisages Governmental financial support for management training " to be carried out in Italy or abroad [and] also for resettlement projects in the native countries".

These projects concerning these above mentioned fields are implemented through "co-financing, parallel financing and contributions related to initiatives of the EEC, the EBRD (European Bank of Reconstruction and Development) and other financial organizations of which Italy is member and which pursue the same purpose of this Law".

In order to train managers for Polish Italian joint-ventures the Italian Institute for Foreign Trade organized in 1990 a training course for 100 Polish managers. To be selected for this course the Polish trainee had to be young (under 35 Years) with a good command of English and knowledge of Italian, and to be interested in creating joint ventures with Italian firms in the following industries: agriculture and food; textile and clothing; footwear and other activities connected with consumer goods production.

During phase I of the programme, 72 candidates attended a course at Warsaw University consisting of an introduction to marketing, management and marketing techniques and Polish legislation on joint ventures. In the second phase of the programme 20 participants were selected to attend a course in Italy (Milan). Participants were chosen on the basis of the demand from Italian firms interested in establishing joint-ventures in Poland. The third phase of the course involves a one month *stage* with an Italian firm involved in a business venture in Poland. After the completion of the *stage* the Polish manager returns to Poland to prepare a pre-feasibility project on the establishment of a joint venture. Finally, a committee in Rome evaluates the presented projects and awards course certificates to the trainees.

The Italian Institute for Foreign Trade is planning to organize training courses for managers in other countries of central and eastern Europe.

9. Netherlands

The Dutch government runs a cooperation programme called "Programma Samenwerking Oost-Europa" (PSO) for Bulgaria, Hungary, former Yugoslavia, Poland, Romania and former Czechoslovakia. Country policy programmes lay down the priority areas on which the projects submitted should concentrate in each particular country. Proposals for projects falling within the terms of the country policy programmes can be submitted to the relevant Ministry. If the project is deemed to fulfil the criteria of the country policy programme, it will be discussed with the relevant authorities in the East European country. Projects upon the Dutch and East European authorities reach an agreement are submitted for approval to the programme coordinator in the country concerned. The final decision is taken in the Netherlands. 100% of the cost can be funded under the PSO.

Dutch companies wishing to invest in eastern Europe or create a joint venture there can apply for subsidies at the Financierings Maatschappij voor Ontwikkelingslanden (FMO), situated in the Hague, which is a semi-government institution providing subsidies to for developing countries, including eastern European countries.

10. Nordic Initiatives

The Nordic Investment Bank provides loans to countries, authorities and companies, inter alia in central and eastern Europe, for the financing of investment projects of nordic interest.

In March 1992, the Nordic countries - Denmark, Finland, Iceland, Norway and Sweden, launched an investment programme for the three Baltic Republics, with a budget of ECU 100 million, which will be managed by the Nordic Investment Bank and the EBRD. The funds will mainly serve for the promotion of Small and Medium-Sized Enterprises (SMEs), the establishment of investment banks, assistance with privatisation, the promotion of ties with Baltic companies as well as aid for investment projects.

Nordiska Investeringsbanken
PB 249, SF - 00171 Helsingfjors
Finland
Tel: 358.018001
Fax: 358.0180 00309

In March 1992, Denmark, Sweden, Norway, Finland, Germany, Russia, Poland and the three Baltic Republics set up a Council of the Baltic Sea States which will act as a forum for cooperation and coordination of policies relating to the environment, energy, political and economic affairs, trade, transport, education, telecommunications, culture and humanitarian aid.

Other Nordic initiatives include the Nordic Environment Corporation (NEFCO), the Nordic Project Export Fund (NoPEF) and the Nordic Industry Fund.

11. *United Kingdom*

The Foreign and Commonwealth Office's "Know How Fund" (KHF), was established in 1989 with a fund for Poland (GBP 25 million, doubled to GBP 50 million later the same year). In 1990 there was an extension of funds to the rest of eastern Europe, but funds are only allocated once the beneficiary country demonstrates that it is fully committed to reform. Consequently, funds for Hungary (1989), Czechoslovakia (1990), Bulgaria (1991) and Romania (1991) was set up. The KHF is individually tailored to each country's needs, but has five priority areas in which funds can be allocated:

- assistance to the financial services sector (advice on privatisation, accountancy and audit, and banking training);
- co-operation between the respective employment services;
- advice on the establishment of small businesses;
- management training;
- and the training of civil servants and local government officials.

To apply for funds under this scheme, an applicant must first of all register an interest to work in eastern Europe. This is essential since all proposals will be put out to competitive tender. The request must come from eastern Europe to the British Embassy in the countries covered by the KHF.

Training for Investment Personnel Scheme (TIPS)

This scheme supports UK businesses which wish to provide training, in particular management training, for key eastern European or CIS personnel who will help to run their investment operations that have just been, or are about to be, established. The scheme is intended to help make up the deficiency of management and business skills in the eastern European and CIS economies generally. UK investing businesses themselves should meet the main cost of training eastern

European or CIS staff. The contribution under the scheme is a grant covering half the actual cost, or a maximum of GBP 50.000. The grant can be paid after the training has been completed and a satisfactory report has been submitted. Eligible businesses must be registered and actively carrying on business in the UK. Applicants may be a subsidiary, or form a part, of a foreign company or international group. The scheme covers UK investment operations currently in the following countries: Poland, Hungary, Czech and Slovak Republics, Bulgaria, Romania and the former Soviet Union. Eligible training activities includes: bringing over a few key eastern European or CIS personnel to the UK for a short period of time; sending one or two trainers or managers from the UK to train personnel on site in one of the countries; or a combination of both. Key personnel need not necessarily be directors or senior managers. The investment as such may, for example, take the form of a joint venture or the establishment of an operating subsidiary. Investment operations comprising only portfolio investment, or relating contracts for the sale or marketing of goods or services however are not eligible.

Pre-Investment Feasibility Studies Scheme (PIFS).

The second scheme is intended to help those UK businesses who have undertaken basic market research, have visited the market and potential investment partners (or have been looking at the prospects of setting up a 100% owned subsidiary) and now have a specific new long-term investment operation in mind. The scheme assists with the cost of determining the commercial and financial viability etc. of that prospective investment. The eligibility of businesses, countries, investments and available grants are equal to the TIPS-scheme.

The Foreign and Commonwealth Office's Know How Fund

Enquiries about the KHF should be made to:

> The Joint Assistance Unit,
> Eastern European Department,
> Foreign and Commonwealth Office,
> King Charles Street,
> London SW1A 2AH, United Kingdom.
> Fax: 071-270 3012

Telephone enquiries regarding a specific country or scheme should be made to:

Poland:	071-270 2944
Hungary, former Czechoslovakia, Bulgaria:	071-270 3470
Romania:	071-270 3559
CIS:	071-270 3565
PIFS and TIPS Schemes:	071-270 3563

Companies requiring information about doing business in eastern Europe, including conditions for investment, should call regarding:

Poland, Bulgaria:	071-215 4734
Hungary:	071-215 5673
Former Czechoslovakia:	071-215 5267
Romania:	071-215 5152
CIS:	071-215 5265 / 4257

12. *United States*

The US Agency for International Development (USAID) administers the US economic and humanitarian assistance program in more than 80 countries worldwide. The Agencys Bureau for Europa is responsible for the administration of the assistance program for central and eastern Europe.

The Management Training and Economics Education Project was initiated in 1991 by USAID's Bureau for Europe and the US Information Agency (USIA) to respond to the lack of a modern system of management education. The 829.5 million project aims to develop the technical, management, and economics skills necessary to restructure central and East European economies and develop competitive markets and businesses.

The project helps develop basic business skills both in the private businesses and large state enterprises scheduled for restructuring or privatization. Emphasis is also placed on strengthening the understanding or market economies among teachers, government officials, and the general public through mass media. Technical assistance is provided through grants to some 32 US colleges and universities working with counterpart institutions in Czech and Slovak Republics, Poland, Hungary, Romania and Bulgaria.

With a USD 1.5 million USAID grant, the University of Delaware, for example, is providing business management training, economics education, and English as a Second Language instruction to economics teachers, policy makers, business managers, and journalist in Bulgaria. The management training component of the program offers management courses for small businesses in a variety of locations throughout the country. Five University of Delaware management faculty taught courses attended by over 500 Bulgarian small business owners during the fall of 1991 in such topics as fundamentals of marketing, and management techniques for small and medium businesses.

The economics education component provides instruction in market-oriented economics to Bulgarian university professors, government economists, and journalists specialising in economic reform. The courses, taught by University of Delaware professors at Sofia University, include economics of private property and privatisation, and economics of the monetary and financial system.

The English language component offered 30 specialized courses in the fall of 1991 academic semester, attended by over 400 businessmen, economists, economics students and journalists. The English for Journalists courses have trained Bulgarian news professionals in western-style techniques. Training in new teaching methods has also been provided for Bulgarian English language teachers in Sofia's leading academic institutions.

With a grant from USAID, the University of Washington and Washington State University are implementing a management training and economics education program in Romania, in close collaboration with the Bucharest Polytechnic Institute and the Academy of Economic Studies -- one of the oldest and largest universities for business training in the country. Small Business Development Centers will be opened at the two Romanian institutions. University faculty will be trained in market economies and in consulting skills to better address the needs of small business and industry clients at these centers. The centers will also provide consulting services to entrepreneurs. Ten American professors will conduct faculty training in accounting, economics, finance, marketing, management and organization. In addition, librarians from the two US universities will work to strengthen the business libraries of the Bucharest Polytechnic Institute and the Academy of Economic Studies.

The University of Minnesota has created two centers for management training in Poland: one at the Warsaw School of Economics, the other at the University of Agriculture and Technology on Olsityn to teach business management, market economics education, production and management and applied technology. Course participants include faculty from Polish Universities, graduate students, managers active in current or soon-to-be private enterprises in the Warsaw area, and officials responsible for the development of policies in the Ministries of Industry and Trade and Agriculture.

USIA has awarded nine small grants under the Management Training and Economics Education project. A USIA grant to the University of Hartford, for example, is providing management education in Poland through the exchange of eight business faculty members with Jagiellonian University. The joint effort will create a business school curriculum, plan a business studies development program, and train faculty.

A western Style MBA program targeted to working professionals is being developed at the Prague School of Economics in conjunction with DePaul University's College of Commerce.

5.3 PRIVATE FUNDS

Belgium

European Foundation for Management Development

Founded in 1971 by the International University Contact for Management Education and the European Association of Management Training Centres, to provide an international network of private and public organizations, educational institutions and individuals for promoting management development.

Activities: Organizes annual activities for particular sections of its membership, and an annual conference on a subject of current and prospective importance for all categories; initiates special studies, meetings, seminars, workshops, and projects on Selected topics; brings relevant issues in the field of management development and education to the attention of national or international representative bodies; sponsors professional associations in specific fields; publishes or sponsors publications for its members. The Foundation has more than 550 members, who are chiefly European, but all the other continents are also represented, and close contact is maintained with international organizations such as the International Labour Office and OECD. The Foundation promotes the creation of national networks of members to facilitate the exchange of information on a national basis and the development on transnational activities. The Foundation administers management training programmes in the People's Republic of China, India, Algeria and in the countries of central and eastern Europe.

Publications: European Management Development Journal (quarterly); reports of principal meetings and on special subjects.

Address: 40 rue Washington, 1050 Brussels; Tel: (2) 648 03 85; Fax: (2) 646 07 68; Telex: 650080.

Germany

Deutscher Akademischer Austauschdienst - DAAD *(German Academic Exchange Service)*

Founded in 1925, the DAAD is a joint organization of institutions of higher education which aims to promote academic exchanges between Germany and other countries.

Activities: Awards scholarships to foreign students and young research workers on an annual basis, including "sur place" scholarships tenable at some universities in developing countries, and to students from European countries for university vacation and language courses. Scholarships are also awarded to German students and research workers and are tenable in almost all countries of the world. Supports a programme of exchanges of university teachers for short-term teaching and research visits on a reciprocal basis. Through the Liaison Office for German University Personnel Abroad requests are met from foreign universities for German academic teaching personnel. The Office supports them financially during during their stay abroad and aids their subsequent re-integration in German academic life. A similar programme is administered for lecturers in German language and literature. Participates in an international trainee exchange programme for German and foreign students who are given the opportunity to receive practical training in industry, public services and research institutes. Short-term fellowships are awarded to foreign academics for study visits in Germany and a large number of study visits of groups of foreign academics and students to Germany are supported. Under the Artist-in-Berlin programme a number of internationally known foreign artists are invited to Berlin every year for periods of six to 12 months. General questions of international academic and scientific relations, such as educational aid for less developed countries, are also dealt with. DAAD maintains branch offices in Cairo, London, Jakarta, Nairobi, New Delhi, New York, Paris, Rio de Janeiro, San José and Tokyo.

Publications: General and specialized study guides, for example for the European countries; *Information Bulletin for German Universities Personnel Abroad.*

Trustees: The Board of Trustees is composed of representatives from various Federal ministries, the State Ministries of Cultural Affairs and Education, university teachers, representatives of student bodies and from other organizations active in the field of higher education. There is a General Assembly composed of the rectors or presidents of the universities and a representative of their student body, and an Executive Committee.

Körber-Stiftung *(Körber Foundation)*

Founded in 1959 by the industrialist Kurt A. Körber. The Foundation sponsors science, research and education; cultural projects and institutions; the welfare of the elderly and sick; environmental protection; and international understanding.

Activities: Within the framework of the Bergedorf Round Table, the Foundation encourages the study of basic technological, economic, social and politico-educational problems of industrial society; it organizes the German Presidents' Award for Student Competition in German History, the Haus im Park Theatre, the Recreation Centre for Senior Citizens, the Fund for the Promotion of the Arts in Bergedorf Schools, and an exchange programme for young workers to promote German-American friendship. It also donates prizes for various causes, including the promotion of young actors.

Address: Kampchaussee 10, 2050 Hamburg 80; Tel: (40) 7217 050; Fax: (40) 7250 3645; Telex: 217 831.

Stiftung Volkswagenwerk (Volkswagen Foundation)

Founded in 1961 by the Federal Republic of Germany and the State of Lower Saxony for the promotion of science, technology and the humanities in research and university teaching.

Activities: Operates nationally and internationally through grants for specific purposes to academic and technical institutions engaged in research and teaching. The Foundation is free to support any area of science, as well as the humanities, but has limited its funding programme to a range of specific fields. In the case of applications from abroad, cooperation with German research workers or scholars is usually essential.

Publications: Annual report of operations and financial statement; *Outlines* (Information in English); *Schriftenreihe der Stiftung Volkswagenwerk.*

Board of Trustees is chaired by Prof. Dr J.-L. Schreiber.

Address: Kastanienallee 35, Postfach 81 05 09, 3000 Hanover 81; Tel: (511) 8381-0; Fax: (511) 8381 344; Telex: 922965.

United Kingdom

Foundation for Management Education

Founded in 1960 to support and make grants to colleges and other institutions at university level for study of business management; to establish professorships, fellowships, lectureships and scholarships; and to provide grants for interchange of staff and students between countries and for dissemination of knowledge.

Activities: Operates nationally and internationally through grants to business schools, universities and colleges for specific projects, and for the exchange of staff and students between countries. No grants are awarded to individuals.

Address: Sun Alliance House, New Inn Hall St, Oxford OX1 2QE; Tel: (865) 251 486; Fax: (865) 723 488.

United States of America

Alfred P. Sloan Foundation

Founded in 1934 for broad charitable purposes.

Activities: Operates mainly nationally in the fields of science and technology, economic affairs, management and related fields through self-conducted programmes and grants to institutions. The Foundation sponsors the Sloan Fellowships for Basic Research for young chemists, physicists, mathematicians, neuroscientists and economists in institutions in the USA and Canada.

Address: 630 Fifth Ave, New York, NY 10111; Tel: (212) 582 0450.

Ford Foundation

Founded in 1936 by Henry Ford and Edsel Ford to advance the public welfare by identifying and contributing to the solution of problems of national and international importance.

Activities: Grants are made primarily to institutions within the Foundation's six major fields of interest: Urban Poverty and the Disadvantaged - including community self-help initiatives, housing rehabilitation, educational and employment programmes, early childhood education, maternal and child health and nutrition, and research on urban problems; Rural Poverty and Resources - including community-based rural development, national policy planning, income-generating projects, improvement of opportunities for women, the landless and migrants, management of resources and environmental problems in the former USSR and eastern Europe; Human Rights and Social Justice - including human rights in the former USSR and eastern Europe, civil rights, sex discrimination, refugee and migrant rights, freedom of expression and opinion, and legal services to the poor; Governance and Public Policy - including projects to promote democracy and civic participation and improve local governments and the non-profit sector; Education and Culture - support for excellence and equity in education, artistic creativity, and cultural preservation in developing countries; International Affairs - conducting research and public education on international peace, security and arms control, international economics, international organizations and law, and foreign-area studies. The Foundation also promotes family planning efforts in the USA and developing countries, as well as research on population change.

Address: 320 East 43rd St, New York, NY 10017; Tel: (212) 573 5000; Fax: (212) 599 4584; Telex: 224048

The Soros Foundation-CIS

Established in 1987. **Donor:** George Soros

Purpose and activities: Support primarily for intercultural relation between the USA and the CIS, including grants awarded to citizens of the CIS and conferences in the USA.

Geographic limitation: Giving primarily in the USA, the CIS and Europe.

Application information: Initial approach: Telephone or letter; Deadline(s): None; Final notification: usually, one month.

Address: 888 Seventh Ave., New York, Ny 10106

The Soros Foundation-Hungary, Inc

Established in 1983 in New York. **Donors:** George Soros; George Soros Charitable Lead Trust; Tivada Charitable lead Trust.

Purpose and activities: Supports Hungarian organizations and projects including the fields of language, culture, and education; also awards grants and scholarships to individuals for higher education and medical research.

Financial Data (Fiscal date: 31.12.90): Assets amount: USD 3,345,080 AM; Contributions received: USD 3,322,149; Expenditures: USD 5,936,311; Qualifying distribution: USD 5,918,123; Total giving: USD 5,391,785; Grants amount: USD 5,255,332 (No. of grants: 142; Highest grant: USD 750,000; Lowest grant: USD 15; Average grant: 2,000-20,000); Scholarship amount: USD 136,453 (No. of Scholarships: 119; Highest scholarship: USD 7,000; Lowest scholarship: USD 65).

Grantmaking programmes:

Competitions Programmes: The foundation supports numerous competitions, primarily in education. These competitions include a competition to reform both the structure and the curricula of Hungary's liberal arts universities; a Social Science Competition to encourage university students in certain scientific research areas; a Summer Programme for Teachers of English to promote professionalism in the teaching of the English language in Hungary through participation in a six-week summer programme in the USA; a Natural Language Competition for Hungarian students to attend Choate Rosemary Hall; and a competition to support democratic organizations.

Soros Scholarships: The General Scholarship Programme is designed to accommodate individual needs and aspirations. Scholars may apply to study in any western country for a period of up to ten months. A screening committee in Budapest forwards selected applications to New York, where an American academic committee, set up by the foundation, awards the scholarships. In the Oxford Postgraduate and Postdoctoral Scholarship Programmes, the foundation enables Hungarian scholars working on their doctoral theses to attend the University of Oxford. In an agreement with the University, the foundation holds competitions in all areas of research. Applications are screened by a foundation committee, and final selections are made by an expert panel from Oxford.

University Exchange Programmes: The foundation supports several exchange programmes between Hungarian, English and American colleges and universities. The programmes are usually arranged by the participating institutions themselves, and tuition, room and board is usually waived. The foundation provides travel and personal expenses for the participating Hungarian students, who are selected by their schools based on openly-announced competitions and under the guidelines and supervision of the foundation. The foundation remains interested in increasing the number of exchange programmes in the future.

University Scholarship Programmes: The Catholic University of Leuvens Scholarship Programme awards scholarships based on announced competitions in specific research areas. The Indiana University-Bloomington Scholarship Programme affords young scholars the opportunity to pursue American or Jewish studies. In an arrangement with the foundation, the university evaluates all finalists. Th Rutgers University Scholarship Programme accepts scholars for postgraduate study.

Geographic limitation: Giving primarily in Hungary.

Governing body/executive staff: <u>Governing and Directors</u>: George Soros (Pres.);   Philip Kaiser (Vice-Pres.);   William D. Zabel (Vice-Pres.);   Elizabeth Lorant (Exec. Dir.); Wassily Leontief. <u>Staff</u>: 6.

Application information: Copies of proposal: 1;   Deadline: None;   Board meeting dates: Usually within 1 month. <u>Write</u>: Elizabeth Lorant (Exec. Dir.); James McLain (Prof. Officer); or Eva Zorandy (Prog. Officer).

Address: 888 Seventh Ave., Suite 1901, New York, Ny 10106; Tel: (212) 757 2323.

6. USEFUL INFORMATION

6.1 ADDRESSES AND CONTACTS RELATED TO MANAGEMENT TRAINING AND CONSULTING INSTITUTIONS

CZECH REPUBLIC

Institute of Foreign Trade: Director: Brdek Miroslav
Te. Politickych Véznu 10
1010 PRAHA 1
Tel: 235 9871
Fax: 232 2868 or 232 2861.

ESTONIA

Estonian Small Business Association: Chairman: Riivo Sinijarv
Consiori 29, Suite 130
TALLIN EE 0104
Tel: (7-0142) 430 677 or 431 251 or 421 484
Fax: (7-0142) 422 279.

FRANCE

Institut Supérieur de Gestion: Director: Dominique Bernard
6.8, rue de Lota
75116 PARIS
Tel: (33.1) 45.53.60.00
Fax: (33.1) 47.55.96.31.

POLAND

Scientific Society for Organization and Management: President: Prof. Henryk Sadownik
ul. Koszykowa 6
00-564 Warszawa
Tel: 29 99 73 or 29 21 27.

UNITED KINGDOM

International Management Research and Innovation Centre: Dr. Carla Millar
Thames Polytechnic
Bexley Road
Eltham
LONDON SE9 2PQ.

UNITED STATES

Arthur D. Little
Management Education Institute
Admissions Office
35 Acorn Park
CAMBRIDGE, Massachussets 02140-2390
Tel: (617) 498 6200
Fax: (617) 498 7100
Telex: 921 436

EUROPEAN ECONOMIC COMMUNITY (EEC)

Commission of the EEC
Directorate General for External Relations (DG1)
PHARE Operational Service
Mr. Peter Kalbe
84, Rue de la Loi
BRUSSELS 1049
Tel: (32 2) 236 4251
Fax: (32 2) 235 0026 / 236 1951

For details on the **PHARE** programme, contact should be made with the Programme Management Units (PMU's) concerned:

1. **Bulgaria**
   Ministry of Industry and Trade
   29, Aksakov Str.
   SOFIA 1046
   Assistant to the Minister
   Tel: (359 2) 871 914
   Fax: (359 2) 871 915

2. **Hungary**
   State Property Agency
   Pf 708
   1399 BUDAPEST
   The Managing Director
   Tel: (361) 111 0200
   Fax: (361) 111 6037

3. **Poland**
   (i) Privatisation.
       Foundation for Privatisation
       36 Krucza Street
       WARSAW
       The Managing Director.
       Tel: (482 2) 628 2198 or 628 2199
       Fax: (482 2) 625 1114

   (ii) Restructuring.
       Industrial Development Agency
       4 Wsponia Street
       WARSAW 00 926
       The Executive Director
       Tel: (482 2) 628 0934
       Fax: (482 2) 628 2363

4. Romania

National Agency for Privatisation
Str. Ministerului 2-4
Secteur 1, Cod 70109
BUCHAREST
The Executive Director.
Tel: (400) 136 136
Fax: (400) 156 015

National Coordinators of Overall **PHARE** Programmes (for those countries where PMU's have not yet been set up) should be contacted regarding countries so far not mentioned:

Bureau for Coordination of Foreign Assistance: President: Mr. Zdenek Drabek
NAB. KPT. JAROSE 1000
17032 PRAGUE 7
Czech Republic
Tel: (422) 389 1111
Fax: (422) 375 641

ANNEXES

ANNEX 1

MAIN CONCLUSIONS OF THE WORKSHOP ON THE MANAGEMENT OF EAST-WEST JOINT VENTURES, AUSTRIAN FEDERAL ECONOMIC CHAMBER, VIENNA, AUSTRIA, 24 MAY 1991

At the 39th session of the Committee for Trade (3-5 December 1990), the delegation of Austria informed the Committee that the Federal Economic Chamber of Austria proposed to organize a Workshop on "Management of East-West Joint Ventures" in cooperation with the Economic Commission for Europe. The Workshop took place on 21 May 1991 at the Federal Economic Chamber, Vienna, Austria.

The purpose of the Workshop was:

- to compare and asses the experience relating to the management of joint ventures as well as relevant information from enterprises contemplating establishing such ventures in the countries in transition;

- to engage in an exchange of views with management-training practitioners who are currently assisting joint ventures and management personnel to overcome the difficulties mentioned above, and;

- to formulate proposals or recommendations which could be carried out by enterprises and training establishments with a view to overcoming management deficiencies in joint ventures.

Summary of the main points

Participants highlighted the communication problem in East-West Joint Ventures which had arisen from the differences in management culture from both the East and West perspective. Western managers expressed concern that their eastern European counterparts displayed little commitment to the enterprise and appeared to think only in the short-term. Dissatisfaction was further conveyed at eastern European managers' unwillingness to be in command personally, to take decisions or to find solutions to problems. In addition, western managers expressed concern with the perceived authoritarian management style which is still inherent in their joint venture partners' decision making. On the other hand, eastern European managers indicated their unhappiness both at the way their Western counterparts treated them as well as at the latter's lack of understanding with their predicament.

Participants believed that these cultural differences were due to the fact that managers had been brought up in two very different economic systems. Friction arose due to these cultural differences and also to the great insecurity of East European managers with respect to their professional future. It was however felt that these differences could be bridged over time but, in the meantime, Western managers should take care not to adopt the role of "missionaries" in the countries in transition since such behaviour would only create resentment and inflexibility and would increase resistance to change.

With regard to the ideal management profile for East-West Joint Ventures, participants distinguished between a manager's personal qualities and his skills. Participants felt that the most important qualities required was the ability to motivate, take risks, and make decisions. Qualities associated with the ability to communicate and to build teams were also stressed. As to the skills required, these depended on the type of business operation being planned in the economies in transition. Many of the representatives of Western companies present said that plans were underway to expand and develop operations in the economies in transition. Thus, not only would more managers be required but also managers capable of managing a more extensive and sophisticated range of operations. Reflecting their own business activities in the economies in transition, participants identified several types of joint venture: sales and engineering; finance and accounting; production; and services. Management skills would be required in all these fields. Marketing, accounting and human resource managers were all identified as playing a key role in joint venture operations.

Furthermore, participants noted that in joint ventures which had been established recently and where the eastern partner is seeking assistance from the western partner in restructuring its business to prepare it for the market economy, managers of joint ventures will now have to be competent in dealing with key problems affecting the company's competitiveness and its chances for survival, involving, inter alia, its liquidity, over-staffing and over-diversification, threats to its foreign markets and increased competition in its home markets.

Participants stated that managers in eastern Europe and the former Soviet Union often had a good educational background, displayed a keen willingness to learn (especially younger managers) and possessed excellent engineering and science skills on a par with those in the post advanced western countries. These countries also excelled in areas such as software design and engineering.

On the other hand, participants felt that available management resources were insufficient, qualitatively and quantitatively, to meet the requirements and challenges facing new East-West Joint Ventures. There were few managers with the necessary leadership qualities to take motivate subordinates. In particular, participants emphasized the lack of skills in finance and accounting, marketing and sales and in human resources management, and the lack of managers who understood basic market concepts such as"shareholder" or "balance sheet".

Participants discussed some of the methods - training and other means - which they had used to overcome these shortages in qualified management. For representatives of large companies the main method in the training field was to bring their eastern European managers to company headquarters, other subsidiaries worldwide, or to their own training schools. For smaller companies with less resources enterprises had opted for on-the-job training, usually binging in western staff to teach managers on the job. Companies had also used western business schools to provide short courses for their eastern European managers. While these training schemes were being set up, companies have favoured using expatiates to manage their joint ventures (often citizens of the economies in transition who had gained most of their business experience working in a market economy), or have used retired western executive to take over projects in eastern Europe and to train local managers with a view to them eventually taking charge of the business.

Participants, found however, that none of these methods offered a fully satisfactory solution to their problem of finding qualified managers. There was, for example, little confidence that the t aini g methods they had chosen were working. Some companies found that training older East European managers had been a waste of time. In some cases newly trained managers left to join other joint ventures. Western-style business courses were often not appropriate to teach managers brought up in command economies. East European managers were also known to treat short-term training in Western business schools as tourist-breaks rather than as opportunities for serious learning. Other methods also had their problems. Some companies found that expatriate managers who were originally citizens of the country often met considerable local resentment on their return. Also, it was recognized that in general, western expatriate managers were not interested in relocating to eastern Europe and especially to the former Soviet Union.

Participants emphasized the desirability of an evaluation of the various training approaches. Until this was done there was a risk that funding, either from Government or private sources, would not be used properly. Each country, it was stressed, had its own identity. Thus, it was not possible to devise training models which would work for all the economies in transition. Participants believed that the long-term solution lay in developing training programmes in the countries concerned and, in particular, in raising standards and developing business schools in the economies in transition. It was emphasized that western management schools could play an important role in training western European trainers. Some management training specialists, however, stressed that "training the trainers" required not only short-term courses but also the building of longer-term links between eastern and western management schools, teacher exchanges and joint research between trainers in East and West, before concrete benefits could be expected.

Recommendations: Participants emphasized the need for assistance and coordinated action by appropriate international agencies to provide, regular up-to-date information on the following:

- government funding (at the multilateral and bilateral levels) to assist in the costs of management training in eastern Europe;
- availability of training programmes in the western and eastern Europe;
- an evaluation of the various training approaches to the management problem, so that enterprises might be advised on how to use their funds to the best effect.

MAIN CONCLUSIONS OF THE WORKSHOP ON THE MANAGEMENT OF EAST-WEST JOINT VENTURES, ITALIAN INSTITUTE OF FOREIGN TRADE, ROME, ITALY, 8 July 1992

The workshop represented the second in a series to address the problem of the lack of suitably trained managerial personnel for joint ventures and foreign direct investment projects in the countries of central and eastern Europe. The Italian Institute for Foreign Trade, which takes part in the Italian delegation to the ECE's Working Party on International Contract Practices in Industry and is currently concerned with several matters related to East-West joint ventures, offered to host a follow-up workshop and at which progress in finding solutions to the problem of recruiting and training effective managers could be assessed.

The problem faced by western firms trying to establish business operations in eastern Europe -the lack of managers in eastern Europe with both the knowledge and the capacity to operate an enterprise in a market environment - was addressed by various speakers. They noted that central planning to varying degrees had produced a particular type of manager whose value system was quite different from that of western managers. For example, it was pointed out that eastern European managers in contrast to their western counterparts have tended to shun taking decisions, be averse from assuming authority or taking risks, etc. In approaching production the value system of the eastern manager has particularly stressed quantity or sheer output whereas in the west the manager puts more emphasis on quality, sales and marketing. In addition, as the functions of marketing and finance had traditionally been provided for managers by the state ministry, eastern European managers could in the past safely ignore the crucial concerns of western managers such as the quality, cost and delivery times of their products. Speakers took the view that the most urgent management training needs in eastern Europe today are: in restructuring; valuation; accounting; marketing; and quality management.

In discussing both the number and type of manager required for East-West foreign investment projects, it was noted that not only a larger number of joint ventures is being established - over 40,000 according to the latest data from the ECE data base - but that their functions are changing from being typically selling or trading companies aimed at the eastern market to large scale manufacturing. As indicated by several speakers, already many of the firms acquired by western companies under privatization are being integrated into the acquiring company's multinational manufacturing network. These companies are thus manufacturing goods for western markets. All this means that increasingly versatile and competent managers are required for East-West joint ventures, undertaking more sophisticated functions: production, hiring, firing, restructuring, etc. and working to higher western standards of product quality and safety.

Speakers also noted a problem on the supply side where little is presently being done to reorient management training in eastern Europe. Several speakers noted that while many new training institutes were being set up all over eastern Europe, most were of doubtful quality and trainers for the most part have no experience or knowledge about management in a market economy. Also, while there was growing links between western and eastern schools and assistance at the international level to encourage academic exchange most speakers believed that this was not sufficient to offset the other problems faced in these countries - namely the decline in central political authority, the precarious financial situation and the difficulties in developing exchanges between western and eastern training institutions.

Representatives of western companies stated that to overcome these deficiencies in management in eastern Europe they initially had to rely on expatriate managers. As much as they would have liked to recruit locally, several businessmen argued, they had to accept that the running of their plants in eastern Europe could not be left to local managers. Expatriate managers were placed in the top posts in the new company, appointed to the new marketing departments and to ensure that the concept of cost and quality were applied to manufacturing operations.

Representatives of western companies described how they have also held training programmes within the company either in the host or the home country for many middle management positions. In most cases eastern European managers were put under the direct supervision of their western counterparts in order to learn how to undertake the tasks they would be doing in the east. According to speakers, this training took place before the company begins production and, depending on the company, can last from three months to a year. From the descriptions of these in-company training programmes it is clear that they can involve large numbers of western managers many of whom have no previous experience of training other managers. One speaker noted how the company's entire management staff in Milan - all 12 managers - taught their own particular functions to 12 managers brought over from Belarus.

Some larger firms described their use of western management schools to send their eastern European managers for short training courses. But this solution was not as widely favoured as using their own company programmes. Nor was there much evidence to date of firms using eastern European training institutes for these purposes.

Training is only one of the ways in which eastern European managers' work is changed under the new owners. According to speakers, western companies also reorganize production in plants in eastern Europe in order to create more effective managers. According to some speakers, western firms find managers suffering from a lack of motivation and a deep pessimism brought on by the fear that their traditional roles within the factory have disappeared. In response, western companies introduce a new system particularly for middle management designed to give them greater authority and decision-taking power. Clear lines of authority are drawn and the old system of group and collective responsibility is scrapped. Also the system of incentives which previously had given rewards in a purely arbitrary way is reformed to ensure that managers are paid for performance. In addition, companies find that in comparison to their operations in the west, there are often too many managers employed in the plant and efforts are made to reduce the management payroll.

Speakers from business admitted that some of these approaches had met with less than the desired success. Expatriates have often been resented by local management and they have found it difficult to integrate into local management networks. In-company training has often proved unsuccessful. Problems arise where the existing management is sent for training without having determined if they are suitable and willing to accept new ideas. One speaker admitted to sending all his eastern European managers on a course in the West and then having to get rid of them all after they came back when it became apparent that none had accepted the new ideas. There has also been a communication problem. Western managers have each had to use interpreters to explain their own company practice to their eastern counterparts. In one small italian company each manager in charge of a particular function had to teach his function within the company to the eastern European manager through an interpreter.

Most speakers were critical of the very short courses that western management schools typically provide eastern European managers. In most cases, according to one speaker, students who go to the west for training leave barely with an appreciation of the classroom. They have not the time and linguistic skills, etc. to acquire much knowledge of management practices in a market economy. Many such courses are also not effective because the designers of the programme themselves lack an appreciation of the values and culture of eastern European management systems.

Until recently it had not been an option to use local training facilities to train managers or to recruit suitable managers for business ventures but several speakers argued that this was beginning to change. Useful training establishments in eastern Europe are emerging despite resource and other problems and some of the best of these establishments are beginning to make an impression.

Many of these schools, speakers reported, are changing as a result of new intakes. Students which barely a year ago were recruited predominantly from the state sector are now coming from the new private or semi-private sector. Moreover, whereas previously the vast majority of students attending courses were over 35, the tendency has been virtually reversed.

Some recommendations for training eastern European managers

The following are some of the main suggestions and recommendations that were made at this workshop:

(a) In the start-up phase western companies should use their own managers to train their counterparts from eastern Europe rather than opt for some form of external assistance e.g. School or consultants. At this stage it is very important when the manager from eastern Europe lacks any background knowledge about the company and its strategy that he acquires the experience of seeing his job being done under actual operating conditions.

(b) Old courses and programmes are not appropriate for training managers for the new eastern Europe. Programmes must be adapted to the new reality whether the providers are companies or schools.

(c) It is important to select with care those managers who require training. Older managers brought up under central planning systems will be extremely difficult to re-train. Those companies which do select managers to send for training usually pick younger managers, since it is assumed that such managers will be more receptive to new ideas.

(d) Actual training of managers should be done wherever possible by an eastern European trainer. As a rule effective training takes place where the teacher and student share the same cultural values, background and language. Future strategies of foreign assistance in management development in the economies in transition should therefore concentrate on training managers in recipient countries.

(e) If choosing an eastern European training establishment to send its managers a western firm should bear in mind the following three criteria in order to select the best: that it has a well-trained faculty; has close links with a western management training establishment; and it has good links with business. Unfortunately, very few eastern European establishments can meet these three conditions at present.

(f) Western firms should take a closer look at the availability of training in the countries where they have established business operations. They should consider recruiting their managers from these new institutions. Western companies should, for example: become actively involved in the development of these business schools; join the board of governors; offer teaching and internship possibilities to student and faculty; and comment on the course design and syllabus.

(g) Because of cost considerations, language barriers, and lack of knowledge about eastern Europe western management schools can only play a minor role in meeting the very large need for management education. Strong local institutions able to provide excellent undergraduate, MBA and executive programmes, must be developed. However, in order to achieve this, western establishments can play a significant role in transferring knowledge to the trainers in eastern Europe. Already the western academic community has taken some steps to forge links with eastern Europe, but much more needs to be done particularly with regard to institutions lying outside the main cities. The ties should be long-lasting. "Training-the- trainer" programmes which sound straightforward are, in fact, difficult to structure effectively and results are not obtained overnight. Western schools also need to be active in accrediting the new emerging management training establishments in eastern Europe.

(h) Representatives of western companies experienced in business dealings in eastern European countries should be involved in the discussions between eastern and western training establishments, be ready to define their management needs and should support the establishment of contacts and exchanges between east and western training establishments.

BIBLIOGRAPHY

Adamiec, J.: *Sociétés Mixtes en Europe de l'Est*, in **Revue d'Études Comparatives Est-Ouest** (Paris, Mar. 1991).

American Management Association: *Doing Business with the Soviet Union* (New York, 1988).

Birenbaum, D.E.; Kachdan, A.; Racklin, D.P.; Thompson, P.G.: *Venturing in the USSR, Hungary and Poland: The Emerging Legal Framework* (New York, Fried, Frank, Harris Shriver and Jacobson, 1990).

Collins, T.M.; Doorley, T.L.: *Teaming Up for the 90s: A Guide to International Joint Ventures and Strategic Alliances* (Homewood Il., Business One Irwin, 1991).

European Communities: *Partnership between Small and Large Firms: Proceedings of the Conference held in Brussels, 13 and 14 June 1988* (London, Graham and Trotman, 1989).

Csaki, G.: *East-West Corporate Joint Ventures: Promises and Disappointments* (Budapest, Magyar Tudomanyos Akademia, 1992).

Franceze, A.: *Tourisme en URSS: Une Industrie à Développer*, in **Courrier des Pays de l'Est** (Paris, Jul.-Aug. 1990).

Geringer, J.M.: *Joint Venture Partner Selection: Strategies for Developed Countries* (New York, Quorum Books, 1988).

Harvard University: *From Marxism to Marketing: Central and Eastern European Students at Harvard Business School*, in **Harvard Business School Bulletin** (Boston, Feb. 1992).

Herlach, M.D.; Barale, L.A.: *Joint Ventures in Eastern Europe* (London, Euromoney Publications, 1990).

Harrigan, K.R.: *Managing for Joint Venture Success* (Lexington, Mass., Lexington Books, 1986).

Hertzfeld, J.M.: *Joint Ventures: Saving the Soviets from Perestroika*, in **Harvard Business Review** (Boston, Jan.-Feb. 1991).

ILO: *State Enterprise Opens Door to Outside Shareholders*, in **Social and Labour Bulletin** (Geneva, Jan. 1988), pp. 16-17.

ILO: *Union Role in Joint Ventures*, in **Social and Labour Bulletin** (Geneva, Oct. 1987), pp.583-584.

ILO: *Right to Hire and Fire Reconfirmed for Foreign investors*, in **Social and Labour Bulletin** (Geneva, Jul. 1987), p. 228.

Kavass, I.I.; Griffin, A.: *Joint Ventures in the Soviet Union: A Review of Current Literature in English*, in **International Journal of Legal Information** (Washington, Winter 1990).

Kirk, M.E.: *Where Walls Once Stood: US Responses to New Opportunities for Academic Cooperation with Eastern-Central Europe* (Washington, East-Central Europe Information Exchange Institute of International Education, 1992).

Kreuzer, K.: *Legal Aspects of International Joint Ventures in Agriculture* (Rome, FAO, 1990).

Kubr, M.: *Management Consulting in Central and Eastern Europe: Challenges and Recent Developments* (Geneva, ILO, 1991) Man Dev/61.

Laky, T.: *Enterprise, Business, Work Partnership and Enterprise Interest* (Budapest, Acta Oeconomica, 1985), pp. 27-49.

Lawrence, P.R.; Vlachoutsicos, C.A.: *Behind the Factory Walls: Decision Making in Soviet and American Enterprises* (Boston, HBS Press, 1990).

McNulty, N.G.: *Management Education in Eastern Europe: Fore and After*, in **Academy of Management Executive**, vol. 6, No. 4 (Washington, 1992).

Morawetz, R.: *Recent Foreign Direct Investment in Eastern Europe: Towards a Possible Role for the Tripartite Declaration of Principles concerning Multinational Enterprises and Social Policy* (Geneva, ILO, 1991).

Prokopenko, J.: *Management Implications of Structural Adjustment* (Geneva, ILO, 1989), Man Dev/54.

Prokopenko, J.; Pavlin, I.: *Entrepreneurship Development in Public Enterprises* (Geneva, ILO, 1990), Management Development Series, No. 29.

Prokopenko, J.: *Human Resources Management in Economies in Transition: The East European Case* (Geneva, ILO, 1992), Management Development Series, No. 66:

Razvigorova, E.; Wolf-Laudon, G.: *East-West Joint Ventures: The New Business Environment* (Oxford, Blackwell, 1991).

Ryssina, V.: *Management Development and Training in European Socialist Countries: Policies, Practices and Prospects* (Geneva, ILO, 1989), Man Dev/50.

Tiraspolsky, A.: *Sociétés Mixtes URSS-Ouest (IV): List Récapitulative et Projets*, in **Courrier des Pays de l'Est** (Paris, Mar. 1988)

Turner, I.: *Transitional Management in Central and European Organizations* (Henley, Henley Management College, HWP No. 12, 1992).

UN: Centre on Transnational Corporations: *Curricula for Accounting Education for East-West Joint Ventures in Centrally Planned Economies* (New York, doc. ST/CTC/SER.B/6, 1990).

UN: Centre on Transnational Corporations: *Joint Ventures as a Form of International Economic Co-operation* (New York, doc. ST/CTC/93, 1988).

UN: Centre on Transnational Corporations: *Challenge of Free Economic Zones in Central and Eastern Europe: International Perspectives* (New York, doc. ST/CTC/108, 1991).

UN: Centre on Transnational Corporations: *Joint Venture Accounting in the USSR: Direction for Change* (New York, doc. ST/CTC/SER.B/7, 1990).

UN: Centre on Transnational Corporations: *Accounting for East-West Joint Ventures* (New York, Workshop on Accounting for East-West Joint Ventures, 1989).

UN: Economic Commission for Europe: *East-West Joint Ventures: Economic, Business, Financial and Legal Aspects* (Geneva, doc. ECE/TRADE/162, 1988)

UNCTAD: *Joint Ventures as a Channel for the Transfer of Technology* (Geneva, 1990).

Vlachoutsicos, C.A.; Lawrence, P.R.: *What We Can't Know about Soviet Management*, in **Harvard Business Review** (Boston, Nov.-Dec. 1990).

Vcherashnaya Rosser, M.: *East-West Joint Ventures in the USSR and China: A Comparative Study*, in **International Journal of Social Economics** (Bradford, 1990).

Zeira, Y.; Shenkar, O.: *Personnel Decision-Making in Wholly-Owned Foreign Subsidiaries and in International Joint Ventures* (Geneva, ILO, 1986).